THE TOP 100
FOODS FOR
A YOUNGER YOU

THE TOP 100
FOODS FOR
A YOUNGER YOU

SARAH MERSON

DUNCAN BAIRD PUBLISHERS

LONDON

The Top 100 Foods for a Younger You
Sarah Merson

Distributed in the USA and Canada by
Sterling Publishing Co., Inc.
387 Park Avenue South
New York, NY 10016-8810

This edition first published in the UK and USA in 2007 by
Duncan Baird Publishers Ltd
Sixth Floor, Castle House
75–76 Wells Street
London W1T 3QH

Managing Editor: Grace Cheetham
Editor: Ingrid Court-Jones
Managing Designer: Suzanne Tuhrim
Designer: Gail Jones
Commissioned photography: Simon Smith and Toby Scott

Library of Congress Cataloging-in-Publication Data Available

ISBN-13: 978-1-84483-394-8   ISBN-10: 1-84483-394-1

10 9 8 7 6 5 4 3 2

Typeset in Helvetica Condensed
Color reproduction by Colourscan, Singapore
Printed in Thailand by Imago

For information about custom editions, special sales, premium and corporate purchases, please
contact Sterling Special Sales Department at 800-805-5489 or specialsales@sterlingpub.com.

Publisher's Note: The information in this book is not intended as a substitute for professional medical treatment and advice. The publishers and author cannot accept responsibility for any damage incurred as a result of any of the therapeutic methods contained in this work. The therapeutic methods contained in this book are intended for adult use only. It is advisable to consult a medical professional before using any of these methods, particularly if you are pregnant, breastfeeding or suffering from a medical condition and are unsure of the suitability of any of the remedies or foods mentioned in this book. All recipes serve four unless otherwise specified.

CONTENTS

KEY TO FOOD BENEFITS

Brain power

Hair, teeth, and nails

Skin

Eyes

Heart and circulation

Musculo-skeletal system

Immune system

Energy levels

Introduction

We're living longer today than ever before. Not only this, but our expectations for health and well-being are also greater. We are no longer willing to accept the inevitability of the aging process—instead, we're striving for a fitter, healthier, and more youthful existence. And, it's not only about *feeling* great, but about *looking* great, too.

For centuries we've accepted that our appearance will deteriorate as the years go by, but science is now proving that the food we eat can put the brakes on the aging process, both on the inside and on the outside. It's long been established that a healthy diet is the cornerstone of a long life, and now we're realizing that it's the key to a youthful life as well. Luckily, eating good food is one of life's great pleasures, and if we invest in a healthy diet now, we can help to prevent ourselves from suffering in later years from ailments such as deteriorating eyesight, arthritis, and heart disease, as well as fatigue, wrinkles, and lackluster skin.

To get the most from our diet, it's vital to

choose food with integrity —fresh, natural, and unadulterated produce is best. By combining fruits, vegetables, nuts, seeds, whole grains, meat, fish, eggs, dairy products, herbs, and spices with plenty of water, we achieve a diet full of life-enhancing nutrients. These give the body the necessary means to keep healthy and to function efficiently, which in turn help us to feel fitter and look younger.

Certain foods, especially fruits and vegetables, are powerful sources of free radical-fighting antioxidants. Many of the visible effects of aging, such as wrinkles, and also those that we can't see, such as deterioration of the heart and eyes, are caused by free radicals— highly reactive molecules

EAT YOURSELF YOUNGER

EAT OR DRINK MORE ...
- **Foods loaded with vitamin C** to counteract free-radical damage and maintain a glowing complexion
- **Selenium-rich foods** to avoid wrinkles, offer protection against damage from the sun, and promote glossy hair
- **Foods containing iron** to prevent lackluster hair and a pale complexion
- **Vitamin B-rich foods** to increase brain power and maintain the nervous system
- **Foods high in calcium** to help to preserve bone health

- **Foods rich in B, C, and E vitamins** to maintain a strong immune system
- **Foods containing zinc** to slow hair loss and promote hair growth
- **Calcium-, magnesium-, boron-, or silica-rich foods** to treat fragile, splitting nails
- **Foods high in vitamin A** to boost immunity and maintain glowing skin, and sparkling, healthy eyes
- **Foods containing silica** for healthy skin, bones, and connective tissue
- **Foods high in vitamin E** for its ability to heal and moisturize the

skin, prevent memory loss, and protect the heart
- **Potassium-rich foods** to reduce high blood pressure and maintain a regular heartbeat
- **Foods high in sulphur (a constituent of keratin and collagen)** to promote healthy skin, nails, and hair
- **Foods with a low glycemic index (GI)** for a sustained release of energy
- **Foods containing omega-3 and omega-6 essential fatty acids** for an alert brain, clear, glowing skin, and protection against heart disease

that damage cell walls and the genetic material within cells. Free radicals are hard to avoid as they're produced naturally in the course of everyday life—factors such as smoking, pollution, and overexposure to sunlight can accelerate their production. However, eating lots of antioxidant-rich fruits and vegetables can be a powerful defence against them and the damage they cause. For example, studies show that eating citrus fruit, which is full of the well-known antioxidant vitamin C, can help to boost the immune system, promote healthy skin and reduce the risk of eye disease. And eating green leafy vegetables, orange sweet potatoes, and apricots and pumpkin, which are all rich in beta-carotene, can help to maintain good eyesight, as well as protect against heart disease.

Foods that are rich in essential fatty acids (EFAs), especially fish, nuts, and seeds also play a vital role in helping us to feel and to look fantastic. Not only do EFAs play a central role in keeping the brain active, the mind agile and the nervous system healthy, but they are also fundamental to the preservation of the elasticity of the skin and to keeping the hair glossy and healthy.

Many other foods and herbs can be used to maintain the skin and the hair in tip-top condition, not only by eating them, but also by using them topically. For example, a milk bath is highly nourishing and helps to keep the skin soft and supple; green tea applied to the area around the eyes helps to reduce sagging, while banana acts as a fantastic hair conditioner.

True, aging is inevitable, but aging gracefully is an art that anyone can master. Armed with the information in this book, you can use everyday foods and herbs to boost your energy levels and improve both your physical and mental performances. This is all achievable in the short term and you will soon see and feel results. In the longer term, you will benefit by staying fitter, feeling better, and looking younger. So don't delay—*now* is the time to invest in your future health and good looks.

FOR A YOUNGER YOU AVOID ...

- junk foods
- sugar
- too much salt
- too much alcohol
- smoking
- stress
- lack of exercise
- lack of sleep

grape

NUTRIENTS
B-vitamins, vitamin C; iron, potassium, selenium, zinc; anthocyanins, flavones, quercetin; fiber

A great source of instant energy, succulent grapes provide all-round protection.

Grapes contain an enormous number of compounds that are uniquely nourishing, thus giving them a reputation as a food for convalescents. This aromatic fruit can prevent and help to treat any number of age-related conditions, from anemia and fatigue to arthritis, varicose veins, and rheumatism.

GRAPE JUICE

6lb. ripe black grapes
piece of cheesecloth

Wash the grapes and collect them in a large pan. Mash them so that the juice begins to flow. Cover them with water and bring to a boil, then reduce to simmer 10 minutes. Mash them again, breaking up as many grapes as possible. Then, secure the cheesecloth over another pan and pour the juice through it. Let juice stand overnight. Remove cheesecloth and drink.

HELP FOR THE HEART

Full of powerful antioxidants, including astringent tannins, flavones, and anthocyanins, grapes help to prevent "bad" LDL cholesterol from oxidizing and blood from clotting, and therefore protect the heart and the circulatory system. High in both water and fiber, grapes are a great aid for detoxifying the gut and the liver. Black grapes also contain quercetin, which helps to minimize inflammation, aiding the cardiovascular system further, as well as promoting healthy digestion.

Since the earliest times, grapes have been dried to make raisins. Dynamos of concentrated nutrients, raisins are full of fiber and are an exceptionally high-energy food. They are also rich in the minerals iron, potassium, selenium, and zinc. Selenium, in particular, is a very important anti-aging nutrient, offering protection from heart disease and boosting the immune system. In addition, selenium helps the skin by keeping fine lines and wrinkles at bay.

GRAPE FACE CREAM

handful of grapes
1 tbsp. fresh heavy cream
½ tsp. lemon juice

Crush the grapes with a fork and press through a strainer to extract 1 tablespoonful of juice. Beat the cream and grape juice together to form a light, fluffy cream. Add the lemon juice gradually, stirring gently and mixing well. Apply to the face and neck. Leave 10 minutes, then rinse off with warm water.

002

mango

High in vitamin C and beta-carotene, mangoes protect against premature aging in many ways.

NUTRIENTS
Vitamins C, E, beta-carotene; fiber

An average-size mango contains an excellent amount of the antioxidant vitamin C, which produces collagen—a protein central to healthy skin and connective tissue. Mango is also one of the few fruit sources of vitamin E, which together with vitamin C, protects the brain from memory loss. With bright orange-yellow flesh, mangoes are high in beta-carotene, which is needed for clear skin, healthy lungs, a strong heart, and good overall immunity.

MANGO LASSI

2 cups plain yogurt
1½ mangoes, peeled and sliced
¼ cup sugar
8 ice cubes
4 pistachios, shelled
4 almonds
pinch of saffron threads

Blend the yogurt, mango, sugar, and ice until frothy. Cut the pistachios and almonds into slivers. Pour the lassi into glasses and decorate with nuts and saffron threads.

003

apricot

With their high carotenoid content, apricots contain a wealth of youth-enhancing nutrients.

Beta-carotene is the most abundant antioxidant found in apricots, helping to protect the skin and lungs from oxidation damage and supporting the immune system. It also prevents free radicals from damaging the eyes. In addition, apricots contain lycopene, one of the most powerful antioxidants. Lycopene is known for its ability to prevent the build-up of fatty deposits in the arteries and it also has strong anti-carcinogenic properties.

NUTRIENTS
B-vitamins, vitamin C, beta-carotene, lycopene; iron; fiber

BRANDIED APRICOTS

4½lb. fresh apricots
bag of cloves
4 cinnamon sticks
6 cups brown sugar
2½ cups vinegar
¼ cup brandy

Wash the apricots and stick 2–3 cloves into each one. In a pan combine the cinnamon sticks, sugar, and vinegar; bring to a boil, and simmer to form a syrup. Put the apricots in the syrup and continue to simmer until soft. Remove from the heat and pack apricots into jars. Add 1 tablespoonful of brandy and a cinnamon stick to each jar, and seal. The apricots will be ready to eat after 14 days.

004

blueberry

Blueberries contain excellent youth-preserving antioxidants, which stave off many conditions.

NUTRIENTS
Vitamins C, E, beta-carotene; anthocyanin, ellagic acid; fiber

Blueberries are popularly known as "brain berries" because they protect the brain from aging.

Blueberries are a rich source of anthocyanin, a potent antioxidant that protects against aging and improves circulation. Anthocyanin also increases the potency of vitamin C, thus supporting collagen and improving the skin. Blueberries help to improve brain function, as well as to fight eye disease. They are also a good source of pectin, which lowers cholesterol levels. Topically, their fruit acid content helps them to act as a gentle astringent and peeling agent.

BLUEBERRY SAUCE

2 cups fresh blueberries
⅓ cup sugar
1 tbsp. fresh lemon juice
pinch of salt
½ tsp. vanilla extract

Wash the blueberries and crush them in a bowl. Add the sugar, lemon juice, and salt. Mix well. In a pan heat the mixture and boil 1 minute. Add the vanilla extract. Serve with desserts, cake, or ice cream. Keeps in the refrigerator 5 days.

papaya

Full of beta-carotene and vitamin C, papaya also contains papain, a powerful anti-aging enzyme.

With plenty of beta-carotene and vitamin C, papaya helps to reduce deterioration of the arteries and lessen the risk of heart disease, as well as fight free radicals. Papaya is also rich in papain, which acts as a wonderful digestive aid that encourages the elimination of waste products. It's also useful for calming inflammation throughout the body. Used topically, papain literally digests dead skin cells and acts as an excellent mild exfoliant.

NUTRIENTS
Vitamin C, beta-carotene, folate; potassium; papain; fiber

PAPAYA EXFOLIATING LOTION *(to brighten and rejuvenate the skin)*

1 large fresh papaya
piece of cheesecloth
1 cup chamomile infusion,
   cooled

Peel the papaya, remove the seeds and purée the flesh in a food processor or blender. Press the purée through a piece of cheesecloth to extract all the juice. Mix the juice with an equal amount of chamomile infusion, and stir well. Using cotton wool balls, apply the lotion to the face and neck, avoiding contact with the eyes. Leave about 10 minutes, then rinse off. Keeps in the refrigerator 2 days.

orange

NUTRIENTS
B-vitamins, vitamin C, carotenoids, folate; potassium; limonene; fiber

As well as vitamin C, oranges contain hesperidin, a key antioxidant for a healthy heart.

Rich in Vitamin C, oranges help to maintain healthy, youthful skin, prevent eye problems, and stop free radicals from clogging up the arteries, a key risk factor for heart disease. Containing the antioxidant hesperidin, oranges are said to protect the heart further by raising healthy HDL cholesterol and lowering "bad" LDL cholesterol. The fruits also contain limonene, which has anti-carcinogenic properties. They provide natural sugars to boost flagging energy levels, are high in fiber and are even reputed to reduce cellulite.

VITAMIN C SMOOTHIE

3 cups freshly squeezed orange juice
3 cups fresh mango chunks
2½ cups fresh strawberries
2½ cups kiwi fruit, chopped
2 cups vanilla yogurt
crushed ice (optional)

Combine all the ingredients in a blender and whizz until smooth. Add ice as required, then pour into tumblers.

cranberry

Cranberries are high in a number of compounds that stave off age-related conditions.

Cranberries contain ellagic acid, which is an antioxidant compound that has been shown to disarm carcinogens, as well as prevent the onset of heart disease. This antioxidant is best absorbed from food in its natural state—good news for those who enjoy eating cranberries. Packed with vitamin C, cranberries are also excellent for keeping the skin and eyes youthful, and for boosting immunity. The berries contain two other ingredients that help to stave off heart disease—the powerful bioflavonoids quercetin and myrcetin.

NUTRIENTS
Vitamin C; iron; ellagic acid; tannins

CHOCOLATE-COVERED CRANBERRIES

2 cups chocolate chips
2 tbsp. butter
3 cups fresh cranberries

Melt the chocolate chips and butter over a low heat, stirring frequently until melted. Using a toothpick, dip the cranberries in the chocolate until they are coated. Lay them out on wax paper. Refrigerate until firm.

008

lemon

NUTRIENTS
Vitamin C, folate; potassium; limonene; fiber

Whether ingested or used topically, lemons provide a wealth of youth-preserving properties.

The high level of vitamin C in lemons means that they are vital for healthy skin and gums. They are also a good source of bioflavonoids, such as quercetin, which boost the effects of vitamin C, and are particularly important for the health of blood vessels and to prevent varicose veins. Lemons, as with other citrus fruits, contain terpenes, which are anti-carcinogenic. When used in beauty treatments, lemon juice inhibits bacterial growth and is astringent, strengthening, and toning.

LEMON TONER
(to treat thread veins)

4 tsp. vegetable glycerin
juice of 1 lemon
1 drop neroli essential oil
1 drop rose essential oil

Mix the vegetable glycerin with the lemon juice and add the essential oils. Apply twice daily to thread veins. Keeps in a sealed jar up to 3 months.

600

banana

One of the most nourishing fruits, bananas contain many important anti-aging nutrients.

NUTRIENTS
Vitamins B3, B5, B6; magnesium, potassium; fiber

Bananas are high in potassium, which keeps blood pressure in check and reduces the risk of heart disease. Potassium works with sodium to maintain the fluid and electrolyte balance in body cells, so bananas help to maintain healthy nerve and muscle function. They have FOS (fructo-oligo-saccharides) to help to feed "good" bacteria in the gut, and aid digestion. They also contain tryptophan, which the body converts to serotonin to aid peaceful sleep.

To ripen bananas, put them in a brown paper bag and keep at room temperature.

BANANA CONDITIONER
(to moisturize dry hair)

1 ripe banana
2 tsp. grapeseed oil

Mash the banana using a fork, then mix with the oil to make a paste. Massage into the hair and scalp, then cover the hair with plastic wrap and leave 30 minutes. Wash out, using a mild shampoo.

prune

Prunes are full of antioxidant power and are great for slowing down the aging process.

NUTRIENTS
Vitamins A, B3, B6; potassium, iron; fiber

Prunes have long been known as a rich source of fiber, but weight for weight, they are the most potent of all antioxidant foods. Their high level of potassium keeps blood pressure in check, while their vitamin B6 protects the heart and boosts brain power. Prunes are also full of iron, providing energy and preventing fatigue. The combination of iron and vitamin A is especially good for hair growth, while vitamin A itself maintains youthful skin and eyes.

PRUNE WHIP

12 large prunes
3 egg whites
3 tbsp. sugar

Preheat the oven to 300°F. Soak the prunes overnight and stew in the soaking water until tender. Remove stones and mash to a smooth pulp. Beat the egg whites until stiff, fold in the sugar and then the prune pulp. Scrape into a greased dish and bake about 20 minutes. Serve with cream.

kiwi fruit

Kiwi fruit contain almost twice as much vitamin C as oranges, and more fiber than apples.

With their high levels of vitamin C, kiwi fruit are a great immunity booster and are particularly good for preserving youthful skin. They are loaded with lutein, a carotene, which, together with vitamins C and E, helps to reduce blood clotting as well as blood fats. Kiwi fruit are also potassium-rich, preventing many age-related conditions from hypertension to insomnia and exhaustion. Their fiber content promotes effective digestion and helps to lower cholesterol.

NUTRIENTS
Vitamins B3, C, E, lutein; potassium; fiber

KIWI FRUIT ICE

4 kiwi fruit, peeled and chopped
2 cups unsweetened apple juice
1 tbsp. lemon juice
½ tsp. grated orange zest

Combine the kiwi fruit, apple juice, and lemon juice in a blender, and whizz until smooth. Stir in the orange zest. Pour mixture into an 8-inch tray and freeze until almost firm. Spoon the frozen mixture into a mixing bowl, and beat until fluffy. Return the mixture to the tray, and freeze again until firm. Leave out at room temperature about 10 minutes before serving.

black currant

Black currants contain a host of powerful anti-aging nutrients, particularly vitamin C.

Black currants are an extraordinary source of vitamin C, containing four times as much as the equivalent weight of oranges. Well-known for attacking free radicals, vitamin C boosts the body's defences, and promotes tissue and cell repair, as well as growth. These tiny berries also contain bioflavonoids, which improve the condition of blood vessels and the skin. In addition, the large amount of potassium in black currants treats water retention and hypertension.

BLACK CURRANT TONER *(to combat wrinkles)*

½ cup black currants
piece of cheesecloth
10 grapes
1 tbsp. fresh lemon juice

Whizz the black currants in a blender and strain them through cheesecloth. Reserve ⅓ cup of the juice. Repeat the procedure with the grapes and save the same amount of juice. Mix together the currant and grape juices, add the lemon juice and pour into a bottle. Apply to the face and neck twice daily with cotton wool balls, leaving to dry naturally. Seal the bottle. Store in the refrigerator 48 hours.

013

blackberry

Plump, sweet, and juicy, blackberries are one of the richest low-fat sources of vitamin E.

Like most berries, blackberries are an excellent source of vitamin C, but what sets them apart is that they also contain good amounts of vitamin E. This helps to neutralize free radicals, which cause heart disease and premature aging of the skin. Blackberries are also a natural source of salicylate, the active substance found in aspirin, which helps the body to fight infection. Some studies have shown that salicylate also has anti-carcinogenic properties.

NUTRIENTS
Vitamins C, E, folate; manganese; salicylate; flavonoids

Add blackberries to your breakfast cereal to help your body to absorb iron from the cereal.

BLACKBERRY AND APPLE FOOL

4 cooking apples
2 tbsp. sugar
2½ cups blackberries
2½ cups bio-yogurt

Peel and slice the apples and put in a pan with the sugar. Heat gently until soft. Stir in the blackberries and cook a further 1–2 minutes. Let the mixture cool, then stir in the yogurt. Chill in the refrigerator.

014

Cantaloupe melon

These succulent summer fruits are bursting with antioxidants to fight aging free radicals.

Cantaloupe melons are very high in vitamin C and beta-carotene, both of which are naturally anti-aging and aid cell repair and growth, as well as supporting the immune and circulatory systems. Cantaloupes also contain potassium, which can lower high blood pressure and "bad" LDL cholesterol. With their high water content, cantaloupes help to detoxify the body.

MELON LOTION
(to cool and hydrate the skin)

¼ **fresh melon, peeled and deseeded**
piece of cheesecloth
½ **lemon**
1 tbsp. olive oil

Whizz the melon in a blender, then filter the juice through the cheesecloth. Squeeze the lemon to extract 1 teaspoonful of juice. Combine the melon juice, lemon juice, and olive oil in a container, cover and store in the refrigerator. Apply twice daily to the face and neck with cotton wool. Keeps in the refrigerator 2 days.

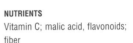

apple

Containing fiber, flavonoids, and vitamin C, apples are a healthy addition to any anti-aging diet.

Apples contain pectin, a fiber that flushes waste products out of the body. It also encourages beneficial bacteria to proliferate in the gut and, with quercetin, helps to keep cholesterol levels down. Apples contain malic acid, too, which relieves rheumatism and arthritis, and assists with energy production. The fruits' vitamin C boosts immunity, while their high water content rehydrates the body.

NUTRIENTS
Vitamin C; malic acid, flavonoids; fiber

Avoid commercial apple juice drinks because they contain high amounts of sugar.

APPLE, PEAR, AND MINT JUICE *(to aid digestion)*

8 apples, cored
8 pears, cored
12 stems of fresh mint

Wash all the fruit, then cut it into chunks, leaving the skin on. Feed through a juicer with the mint. Pour into large glasses and drink immediately.

pineapple

NUTRIENTS
Vitamins B1, B2, C; manganese; bromelain; fiber

Pineapple is particularly rich in bromelain, which helps to reduce inflammation in the body.

Pineapple's main benefits come from bromelain, which is an effective anti-inflammatory, making it exceptionally good for joint problems. Rich in vitamin C, pineapple supports the immune system and defends against free radicals, which can cause premature aging. It's also an excellent source of manganese—an essential co-factor in a number of enzymes important for antioxidant defences and energy production.

PINEAPPLE AND MANGO SALSA

1 large ripe mango
½ small pineapple
¼ red onion
½-inch piece fresh gingerroot, peeled and grated
1 small garlic clove, peeled and crushed
½ small fresh red chili, finely sliced
handful of cilantro, roughly chopped
juice of 2 limes
1 tsp. sesame oil

Peel and chop the flesh of the fruits, then put it in a bowl with the onion, ginger, garlic, chili, and cilantro. Toss well. Drizzle the lime juice and sesame oil on to the mixture. Serve with fish or chicken, or as a dip.

grapefruit

The perfect breakfast food, grapefruit is loaded with antioxidants and is a powerful detoxifier.

Grapefruit is a rich source of youth-preserving vitamin C. The pink variety, in particular, is a good source of potassium and bioflavonoids, both of which are important for the heart and circulation, as well as the skin and immunity. The pectin content helps to eliminate cholesterol from the body. Grapefruit is also rich in alpha-hydroxy-acids (AHAs), which make it an effective toner when used topically.

NUTRIENTS
Vitamin C, beta-carotene, folate, lycopene; potassium; flavonoids; fiber

GRAPEFRUIT BEAUTY MASK (to tone the skin)

1 small grapefruit
1 small pot plain yogurt

Peel the grapefruit and break it into sections. Remove the pith and seeds, and combine with the yogurt in a blender. Whizz to a paste. Put the mixture In a bowl and leave in the refrigerator 1 hour. Apply to the face and leave about 10 minutes. Gently remove with cool water.

strawberry

NUTRIENTS
Vitamins B6, C, folate; ellagic acid

One of the delights of summer, strawberries are full of age-defying nutrients.

STRAWBERRY AND RICOTTA SPREAD

1 cup ripe strawberries
2 limes
2 tsp. confectioners' sugar
⅓ cup ricotta cheese

Mash the strawberries with a fork and grate the zest of the limes. Add the confectioners' sugar and the lime zest and stir well into the ricotta to form a smooth mixture. Spread over toasted cinnamon bagels for a great breakfast treat.

Strawberries are an excellent source of vitamin C, which is essential for the manufacture of collagen—a protein that helps to maintain the structure of the skin. Vitamin C also plays an important role in healing wounds and can ward off gingivitis, the gum disease that affects three out of four adults. Strawberries also contain ellagic acid, a phytochemical that has powerful anti-carcinogenic properties.

Stop strawberries from going soggy by hulling them immediately after washing them.

raspberry

Raspberries are loaded with vitamin C and many potent antioxidants that keep us young.

The high vitamin C content in raspberries boosts immunity and can help to prevent everything from heart disease to eye problems. The fruits also contain ellagic acid, which is anti-carcinogenic and prevents adverse cellular changes. The anthocyanins in raspberries have anti-inflammatory properties, thus protecting from conditions such as arthritis. Raspberries are also effective in combating a number of viruses and bacteria. In addition, they are one of the top fruit sources of fiber, therefore improving digestion.

NUTRIENTS
Vitamins B3, C, folate; iron, manganese; flavonoids, anthocyanins; fiber

RASPBERRY SYLLABUB

1½ cups raspberries
⅔ cup dry sherry, or dry
  white wine
2 tbsp. brandy
grated zest of 1 orange
grated zest of ½ lemon
⅓ cup sugar
2 cups heavy cream

Crush the raspberries slightly (leaving 2 handfuls aside for serving) and mix in a bowl with the other ingredients except the cream. Macerate 4 hours, then force the mixture through a strainer. Add the cream and whip to soft peaks. Put the reserved raspberries in serving glasses; top with mixture and chill. Serve with lace roll-up cookies.

fig

Figs are a fabulous source of fiber. They also add relatively rare vitamin B6 to the diet.

High in fiber, figs can encourage the elimination of toxins and help to lower the risk of heart disease. They are a good source of potassium, which is crucial for controlling blood pressure and lowering the risk of developing heart conditions. Figs also provide useful amounts of vitamin B6, without which we can suffer from a poor memory and increased stress levels.

FIGS STUFFED WITH ORANGE-ANISE CREAM

16 dried figs
½ cup cream cheese, at room temperature
1 tbsp. fresh orange juice
2 tsp. grated orange zest
1½ tsp. honey
½ tsp. anise seed, crushed

Trim and discard the stems from the figs. Cut an "X" down through the stem ends and gently push each fig open. In a bowl combine the cream cheese, orange juice, orange rind, honey, and anise seed. Beat until creamy. Spoon a little mixture into each fig. Keeps in the refrigerator up to 2 hours.

pomegranate

Pomegranates are one of the most powerful sources of antioxidants among fruits.

Extremely high in ellagic acid, pomegranates have anti-carcinogenic and anti-heart disease properties. Antioxidants in pomegranates protect against free-radical damage, including to the skin, and also keep the arteries clear. The antioxidant chemicals also help to protect the skin from sun damage.

NUTRIENTS
Vitamins B1, B3, C; calcium, phosphorus; ellagic acid

POMEGRANATE PUNCH

5 or 6 pomegranates
1 cup sugar
2 cups water
1 cup fresh orange juice
¼ cup fresh lemon juice
1 qt. ginger ale

Cut the pomegranates in half. Scoop out the seeds and put them through a juicer. In a large pitcher dissolve the sugar in the water by stirring rapidly. Add the juiced pomegranate, orange, and lemon juices, then the ginger ale. Chill in the refrigerator and serve.

cherry

Cherries are packed with antioxidants that have amazing anti-aging properties.

NUTRIENTS
Vitamin C; potassium; quercetin, anthocyanins, ellagic acid

Cherries are rich in flavonoids such as anthocyanins, which the body uses to help boost immunity. They also contain quercetin, a strong anti-inflammatory substance, which helps to relieve painful joints and protects against eye disease. Cherries are also rich in the phytochemical ellagic acid, which has anti-carcinogenic properties, and vitamin C, which strengthens collagen and maintains healthy-looking skin and hair. In addition, vitamin C aids the fight against viruses and bacteria.

CHERRY ICE CREAM SUNDAE

6 tbsp. caramel ice-cream topping
¼ cup Grand Marnier liqueur
2 cups vanilla ice cream
2 cups cherries, pitted
handful of crushed cookie crumbs

Combine the ice-cream topping and Grand Marnier in a small dish, stirring until smooth. Divide the ice cream among 4 dessert bowls. Top with the cherries, add the sauce and cookie crumbs, and serve.

rhubarb

A vegetable "fruit", rhubarb is a fantastic source of dietary fibre as well as vitamin C and minerals.

NUTRIENTS
Vitamin C; calcium, magnesium, potassium; oxalic acid; fibre

Full of fibre, rhubarb acts as a natural food laxative, keeping the digestive system in good working order and helping to lower cholesterol and prevent heart disease. It's a good source of immunity-supporting vitamin C, which also helps to plump out wrinkles and keep the skin from premature ageing. Rhubarb is high in calcium for the bones, and potassium to keep blood pressure in check and protect the heart. It is also extremely high in water, which helps to keep the body well hydrated.

RHUBARB FROZEN YOGHURT

300g/10½ oz/2 cups stewed
   rhubarb
100g/3½oz/½ cup natural low-fat
   yoghurt
3 tbsp granulated sugar
2 tbsp orange juice

In a food processor purée the stewed rhubarb until smooth.

Blend in the yoghurt, sugar and orange juice. Cover and freeze in a shallow metal pan for 3–4 hours or until almost firm. Break up the mixture and whizz again in the food processor until smooth. Freeze in an airtight container for 1 hour or until the mixture is firm.

avocado

Full of vitamins A, B, C, and E and essential fatty acids, avocado fights free radicals and is highly nourishing for the skin.

Avocado is native to Central America, and is now grown in tropical regions throughout the world.

ANTIOXIDANT POWER

Loaded with vitamins C and E, avocados are excellent for keeping the skin soft, supple, and healthy, and for maintaining glossy hair. They are high in omega-3 fatty acids, thus helping to prevent wrinkles, enhance brain power, and treat arthritic pain. Avocados are also high in oleic acid, the building block for omega-9 fatty acids, which are also excellent for the skin and have anti-inflammatory properties. They have high levels of the antioxidant lutein, which studies have shown help protect against eye problems and cardiovascular disease.

HEART HEALTHY

With their smooth buttery texture, avocados are high in monounsaturated fat, which raises levels of "good" cholesterol while slightly lowering fatty triglycerides, and beta-sitosterol, a phytonutrient that lowers "bad" cholesterol. They're also full of

---

AVOCADO AND BABY SPINACH SALAD

2 ripe avocados, pitted,
   peeled and cubed
16 cherry tomatoes, halved
2 handfuls of baby spinach,
   washed and torn into pieces

For the dressing:
juice of 2 limes
2 tsp. honey
pinch of salt

Make the dressing by combining the ingredients in a pitcher, and shaking well. Put all the salad ingredients in a bowl and coat with the dressing. Mix gently and serve immediately.

fiber, and are a source of linoleic acid, which the body converts to gamma-linolenic acid (GLA), a substance that helps to thin the blood. Avocados are also one of the richest sources of potassium, which is essential for healthy blood pressure and muscle contraction.

AVOCADO FACE PACK
(to rejuvenate tired skin)

1 ripe avocado
1 tsp. clear honey
1 tsp. lemon juice
1 tsp. plain yogurt

Combine all the ingredients in a bowl and mash into a paste. Cover and leave in the refrigerator 30 minutes. Apply the pack to your face and leave 10 minutes before removing with cool water.

beet

Vibrant in color, beets are loaded with nutrients to help us look younger and feel better.

NUTRIENTS
Iron, manganese, potassium, silica; betacyanin; fiber

Containing the powerful antioxidant betacyanin, which gives beets their deep red hue, these vegetables purify the blood and have anti-carcinogenic properties. Research shows that beets boost the body's natural defences in the liver, regenerating immune cells and helping to lower cholesterol levels. In addition, beets contain silica, which is vital for healthy skin, hair, fingernails, ligaments, tendons, and bones.

GINGERED BEETS

4 beets (with tops), scrubbed and chopped
2 tsp. sesame seeds
1 tbsp. light soy sauce
1 tbsp. extra virgin olive oil
1 tbsp. gingerroot, finely chopped
¾ cup shredded carrots

Steam the beets over a high heat 30–40 minutes until tender. Steam the tops 3–4 minutes, until wilted. Meanwhile, toast the sesame seeds in a dry pan until browned. Then, in a bowl, whisk together the soy sauce, olive oil, and ginger, add all the other ingredients and toss well. Serve warm, or as a salad dish.

cucumber

Laden with water, this popular salad vegetable is well known for its skin-healing properties.

NUTRIENTS
Vitamins A, C; magnesium, manganese, potassium, silica; fiber

Used topically, cucumber helps to maintain a youthful appearance, thanks to its hydrating and anti-inflammatory properties. When ingested, the high water and balanced mineral content makes it one of the best diuretics. Cucumbers are a rich source of silica, a mineral needed for healthy skin, bone, and connective tissue. Silica also plays a major role in preventing cardiovascular disease and osteoporosis.

CUCUMBER CLEANSER
(to refresh and revive the skin)

½ **small cucumber**
5 **mint leaves**
¼ **cup milk**
2 **drops grapefruit seed extract**

Peel and chop the cucumber. Remove the mint leaves from their stems and chop. Put both in a food processor with the milk and whizz until smooth. Pour the mixture into a pan and bring to a boil. Reduce heat and simmer 2 minutes, then leave to cool. Pour into a clean bottle and add the grapefruit seed extract. Store in the refrigerator and use within a week.

celery

Containing very few calories, celery aids weight loss and keeps us looking young.

NUTRIENTS
Folate, beta-carotene; potassium

It is believed that we burn more calories chewing, swallowing, and digesting celery, than we get from eating it, making the vegetable popular with dieters. Its high water content acts as a diuretic, helping to eliminate puffy hands, ankles, and feet. Celery is also excellent for the body's detoxifying processes, including cleansing of the liver, which helps to keep skin looking youthful.

4oz. of celery contains only 7 calories, so it's an ideal food for weight watchers

CELERY RAGOUT

1½ tbsp. butter
1 head celery, sliced
4 large carrots, peeled and sliced
1 red onion, sliced

Melt the butter in a pan. Add the vegetables and coat them in the butter. Season to taste. Cover and cook over a very low heat 30–40 minutes, shaking often to avoid sticking. Serve with broiled fish.

028

bell pepper

When fully ripe, bell peppers are a great source of vitamin C and other anti-aging antioxidants.

Peppers are packed with vitamin C, which helps to fight almost every aspect of the aging process, including deterioration of the skin structure and damage to the arteries. Vitamin C is said to quash carcinogenic free radicals, and to protect against memory problems and eye disease. It is also a potent immunity booster. Red bell peppers are a rich source of lycopene, another renowned anti-carcinogenic nutrient.

NUTRIENTS
Vitamin C, beta-carotene, lycopene; fiber

ROAST PEPPER AND BASIL DIP

1 large red bell pepper
½ cup milk
½ tsp. paprika
½ tsp. salt
2 tsp. extra virgin olive oil
2 tsp. cider vinegar
1 tbsp. chopped basil

Preheat the oven to 400°F. Put the whole pepper in a roasting pan in the center of the oven 20–30 minutes, or until the skin goes black. Remove, and let cool. Peel off the skin and remove seed and core. Save any juice. Blend all the ingredients, including the pepper and its juice, in a food processor to a smooth creamy texture. Serve either chilled as a dip, or warm as a sauce.

NUTRIENTS
B-vitamins, vitamin E, folate;
potassium, silica; fiber

parsnip

Parsnip contains a host of nutrients recognized for their youth-promoting and beautifying effects.

Parsnips are a valuable source of potassium, B-vitamins, vitamin E, and trace minerals such as silica, as well as fiber. Potassium reduces hypertension, while folate is anti-carcinogenic. Vitamin E has been dubbed "the fountain of youth" for its heart-protective properties and ability to prevent skin damage from sun exposure. Parsnips' silica content strengthens the skin and all connective tissue.

PARSNIP CURRY

½ white onion, chopped
1 tbsp. extra virgin olive oil
½ tsp. cumin seeds, crushed
1 tsp. chili powder
½ cup water
4 cups cubed parsnips
1 green bell pepper, cut into
thin strips
¼ cup peanuts, chopped

Sauté the onion with the spices in the oil 5–8 minutes. Add the water and parsnips. Bring to a boil, cover, and simmer over a low heat 20–30 minutes until the parsnips are tender but not mushy. Garnish with the pepper strips and the peanuts before serving.

Parsnips retain more nutrients if kept chilled rather than at room temperature.

onion

A cousin of garlic, onion contains powerful antioxidants and is reputed to counter cellulite.

Onions regulate blood pressure and prevent blood cells clumping. They are a rich source of quercetin, which has anti-carcinogenic properties, and they act as an anti-inflammatory. Onions are an excellent source of selenium, which boosts immunity, cleanses the liver, staves off wrinkles, and limits sun damage. They are also a key source of sulphur, a constituent of the building blocks of skin, nails, and hair.

NUTRIENTS
B-vitamins; selenium, sulphur; quercetin

FRENCH ONION SOUP

4 tbsp. extra virgin olive oil
6 cups thinly sliced onions
2 garlic cloves, crushed
2 tbsp. apple juice
5 cups beef broth
1¼ cups dry white wine
salt and pepper, to taste

In a heavy pan heat the oil. Add the onions, garlic, and apple juice, and cook 5–6 minutes, stirring constantly. Reduce the heat and cook about 20 minutes. Pour the broth and wine into the mixture and season with salt and pepper. Bring to a simmer and cook uncovered 1 hour. Pour into bowls and serve.

Belgian endive

Tasty in salads, Belgian endive is a great source of water, which keeps skin youthful and hydrated.

Fiber-rich Belgian endive, also known as witloof chicory, is extremely useful for helping the digestive system to work efficiently by evacuating toxic wastes, including heavy metals, from the body. Endive is almost 94 per cent water, thus it hydrates the body and improves circulation, benefiting all the organs including the skin and the heart. It's also a diuretic and is very low in calories, so it helps with weight loss.

NUTRIENTS
Vitamin C, beta-carotene; calcium, magnesium; fiber

BELGIAN ENDIVES WITH ROQUEFORT SAUCE

4 Belgian endives
½ cup Roquefort cheese, crumbled
scant 1 cup light cream
sprig of fresh thyme

Divide the endive leaves lengthwise and place them in a serving dish, open-side up. Put the Roquefort in a pan, add the cream and stir over low heat until smooth. Pour the sauce over the endive, sprinkle with thyme and serve.

kale

One of the most power-packed vegetables, kale is especially high in anti-aging antioxidants.

Kale is rich in everything from B-vitamins and carotenoids to a host of anti-aging and beautifying trace minerals. Its vitamin B6 and B12 content helps to boost brain power and prevent memory loss. Loaded with beta-carotene, it is also one of the best sources of lutein, a carotenoid that helps to prevent eye disease. Kale is a valuable source of calcium for the bones and silica for the skin, hair, teeth, and nails. Silica also counteracts the negative effects of aluminum in the body.

NUTRIENTS
B-vitamins, vitamins C, E, beta-carotene, folate, lutein; calcium, iron, silica

KALE WITH GARLIC AND PEPPERCORNS

2 cups water
1lb. kale, chopped
2 tbsp. extra virgin olive oil
½ small onion
2 garlic cloves, crushed
½ tsp. sea salt
½ tsp. freshly ground pepper
¼ tsp. crushed red peppercorns

Put the water in a pan and bring to a boil. Add the kale and cook 2 minutes. Drain and press until barely moist. Put the oil in a large pan and sauté the onion and garlic over a low heat 4–5 minutes. Stir in the kale, salt, black pepper, and peppercorns and cook over a medium heat 3–4 minutes. Serve at once.

broccoli

Broccoli is a rich source of youth-preserving beta-carotene and vitamin C.

With high levels of carotenoids, especially beta-carotene, broccoli has powerful anti-carcinogenic properties, and has been associated with lower rates of both heart and eye disease. As broccoli can increase vitamin A in the body, it also helps to improve various skin conditions. It is a great source of vitamin C, which helps to boost immunity. Broccoli contains calcium, which staves off osteoporosis, and fiber, which keeps the digestive system working smoothly.

CHINESE-STYLE BROCCOLI

1¼lb. fresh broccoli
½ cup canned water chestnuts, sliced
2 tbsp. sunflower oil
small piece of gingerroot, peeled and grated
pinch of grated lemon zest
1 tsp. soy sauce
½ cup water
1 chicken bouillon cube

Cut the broccoli into florets. Put the water chestnuts, oil, ginger, and lemon zest in a pan. Heat, add the broccoli and toss 1 minute. Add the rest of the ingredients. Bring to a boil, then cover and simmer 5 minutes. Serve immediately.

spinach

Full of iron, calcium, and magnesium, spinach is vital for looking young and feeling fit.

Perhaps best known for its iron content, spinach is excellent for oxygenating the blood, generating energy, and preventing anemia. Iron is also especially effective at preventing premature hair loss. Spinach is a rich source of calcium and magnesium, which work together to stave off osteoporosis. Magnesium also relaxes and dilates blood vessels and keeps the muscles flexible. The vitamin C in spinach keeps the skin healthy, while lipoic acid helps to maintain the memory.

NUTRIENTS
B-vitamins, vitamin C, carotenoids; calcium, magnesium, zinc; lipoic acid; fiber

SPINACH AND CRISPY BACON SALAD

1lb. bacon strips
4 eggs, hard-cooked and shelled
2 handfuls of pecan nuts, chopped
1lb. fresh spinach, washed

Cook the bacon under a broiler and cut it into bite-size pieces. Slice the eggs and put them in a bowl with the bacon, pecans, and spinach. Toss well to combine. Drizzle with salad dressing and serve.

cabbage

NUTRIENTS
Vitamins B3, C, folate; calcium, potassium, sulphur

Cabbage contains a range of sulphurous substances and other nutrients to keep us young.

Cabbage is rich in sulphur, which protects the liver and has anti-carcinogenic properties. Sometimes referred to as the "beauty mineral", sulphur is a constituent of keratin, which is vital for strong nails and glossy hair, and collagen, which keeps the skin youthful. The vitamin C in cabbage mops up free radicals. It also contains vitamin B3, folate, calcium and potassium.

STIR-FRIED CABBAGE WITH FENNEL SEEDS

1 green cabbage
2 tbsp. balsamic vinegar
1 tsp. fennel seeds
pinch of cayenne pepper
salt and pepper, to taste

Wash the cabbage and shred it into thin strips. Put the balsamic vinegar in a wok and heat until sizzling. Add the cabbage, fennel seeds, cayenne pepper, and salt and pepper. Cook until the cabbage is softened and slightly browned.

tomato

Full of carotenoids, particularly lycopene, tomatoes have unique anti-carcinogenic powers.

Lycopene neutralizes free radicals before they can cause damage, therefore staving off everything from wrinkles to heart attacks. Studies indicate that lycopene could have twice the anti-carcinogenic punch of beta-carotene. Tomatoes are high in vitamin C, which supports connective tissue in the body and boosts immunity. In addition, tomatoes contain a little iron, which is well absorbed when accompanied by vitamin C, and prevents anemia and fatigue.

NUTRIENTS
Vitamins B3, C, E, beta-carotene, lycopene; iron, potassium

SPICY GARDEN COCKTAIL

4 vine-ripened tomatoes
4 small cucumbers
8 celery stalks, with leaves
hot chili sauce, to taste
celery salt, optional
ice cubes

Cut the tomatoes into chunks and the cucumbers into strips. Remove the celery tops from the stalks, reserving 4 to garnish. Feed the tomatoes, cucumbers, and celery stalks through a juicer. Coat the rims of 4 tall glasses with celery salt and pour the juice into the glasses. Add the hot sauce to taste and several ice cubes. Stir well. Garnish with celery tops and serve immediately.

watercress

NUTRIENTS
Vitamins B3, B6, C, carotenoids;
calcium, iron, magnesium; fiber

Watercress is a highly protective food that helps to strengthen immunity and keep us youthful.

Watercress is rich in vitamin C, thus aiding the regeneration of skin cells, keeping the liver healthy and defences strong. It also contains phenethyl isothiocyanate, a chemical that helps the liver to detoxify and is said to neutralize carcinogenic cells. Watercress is a useful source of iodine—essential for the proper functioning of the thyroid, and vitamin B6 to prevent memory loss. Watercress also helps the release of bile from the gall bladder, which is important for the digestion of fat.

WATERCRESS, ENDIVE, AND ORANGE SALAD

**4 heads of Belgian endive
juice of 1 lemon
1 bunch (7oz.) watercress,
  stalks removed
4 oranges, peeled
2 carrots, grated
⅔ cup apple juice**

Slice the endive, place in a large salad bowl and squeeze over the lemon juice to stop it browning. Chop the watercress roughly and cut the oranges into quarters. Combine them in the bowl with the remaining ingredients, season and toss well. Serve immediately.

♥ globe artichoke

Artichokes are a fantastic food for improving digestion and assisting the body to detoxify.

Artichokes contain cynarin, which increases the flow of bile and improves liver function. The result is better digestion and breakdown of all types of fat. Artichoke treats liver and gall bladder disorders, as well as irritable bowel syndrome and nausea. It's also valuable as a diuretic, helping to relieve water retention and hypertensioin. The youth-enhancing antioxidant flavonoids found in artichokes help to keep the arteries healthy.

NUTRIENTS
Vitamins B3, B5, C, biotin, folate; cynarin; iron, potassium, zinc

---

HOT ARTICHOKE DIP WITH PITA BREAD

8 pita breads
1 cup cream cheese
12oz. mozzarella
1 cup mayonnaise
1¼ cups grated Parmesan
1 onion, minced
2 garlic cloves, crushed
2½ cups marinated artichoke
   hearts

Preheat the oven to 350°F. Cut the pita breads into small triangles, and bake on a cookie sheet until crisp. Combine the other ingredients in a food processor and blend. Put mixture in a dish, and cook in the oven 30 minutes. Serve hot with the pita dippers.

sweet potato

Containing vitamins C and E, sweet potatoes are a fantastic youth-preserving food.

Sweet potatoes are extremely rich in antioxidants. They are one of the few foods containing both vitamins C and E, which work synergistically with one another to help to stave off wrinkles, and to preserve the eyes and the memory. Orange sweet potatoes are abundant in beta-carotene, which keeps the skin, eyes, and lungs healthy, and supports the immune system, along with vitamin C. They also contain vitamin B6, which preserves memory and protects the heart.

NUTRIENTS
Vitamins B6, C, E, beta-carotene; iron, potassium; fiber

HERBY SWEET POTATO WEDGES

6 medium sweet potatoes
handful each of fresh oregano
and thyme sprigs
olive oil, to coat
freshly ground black pepper

Preheat the oven to 350°F. Scrub the sweet potatoes and cut them lengthwise into chunky, wedge-shaped pieces. Put them in a baking dish. Break up the herbs and place them with the olive oil and black pepper with the sweet potatoes. Toss well. Bake about 30 minutes until soft. Serve hot.

radish

Part of the Cruciferae family, radishes contain many nutrients to fight premature aging.

NUTRIENTS
Vitamin C, folate; calcium, potassium, selenium, sulphur

Radishes are rich in sulphur, which is essential for youthful, healthy skin, hair, and nails, and also has anti-carcinogenic properties. Assisting the body in ridding itself of toxins, radishes help to treat gall bladder and liver problems, which might cause premature aging. Radishes are also a valuable source of potassium to keep the heart healthy, calcium to help prevent osteoporosis, vitamin C to fight against eye problems, and selenium to boost immunity.

RADISH SLAW

1 bunch (7oz.) radishes, trimmed and coarsely grated
10oz. green cabbage, finely shredded (about 3½ cups)
1 large carrot, coarsely grated
1 small red onion
2 tbsp. fresh lemon juice
½ tsp. sugar
2 tbsp. extra virgin olive oil
handful of fresh cilantro
salt and pepper, to taste

Combine all the ingredients in a bowl and mix well. Store in the refrigerator and use within 2 days.

mushroom

NUTRIENTS
Vitamins B12, E; phosphorus, potassium, selenium; protein

Mushrooms have more protein than most vegetables, as well as vitamin E and selenium.

A rich source of anti-aging vitamin E and selenium, mushrooms help to maintain healthy skin and hair, and protect against heart disease. They also boost immunity and have anti-carcinogenic properties. Mushrooms contain potassium, which is central to heart health, and vitamin B12, which holds off arthritis. Shiitake mushrooms specifically boost immunity, while the reishi variety combat hypertension and asthma, and maitake treat blood pressure and liver disease.

GLAZED SHIITAKE MUSHROOMS

4 cups shiitake mushrooms
1 tsp. canola oil
⅓ cup chicken broth
1 tsp. cornflour
2 tsp. soy sauce
1 tbsp. dry sherry

Wash the mushrooms, discard the stems and slice. In a large pan heat the oil and add the mushrooms and 2 tablespoonfuls of the broth. Cook, stirring often, 5–6 minutes. In a small bowl dissolve the cornflour in the remaining broth. Stir in the soy sauce and sherry; add to the pan. Cook 2 minutes, or until the mushrooms are glazed.

asparagus

A renowned aphrodisiac, asparagus contains Vitamin E to keep the skin and the heart youthful.

NUTRIENTS
Vitamins B3, C, beta-carotene, folate; potassium, zinc; asparagin; flavonoids; fiber

Asparagus is a fantastic source of folate, which is said to prevent damage to the arteries that supply blood to the heart and the brain. Folate has also demonstrated anti-carcinogenic properties. Asparagus contains asparagine, which, along with its high potassium and low sodium content, makes it an excellent diuretic and cleanser. The vegetable is also high in vitamin E to fight wrinkles, protect the heart, and keep the brain young.

BALSAMIC ROASTED ASPARAGUS

1¼lb. large asparagus spears, trimmed
2 tbsp. extra virgin olive oil
sea salt and freshly ground pepper
2 tbsp. balsamic vinegar
finely grated lemon zest, for garnish

Preheat the oven to 400°F. Coat the asparagus spears in the olive oil and season with salt and pepper. Roast on foil on a baking sheet 20–25 minutes, turning them 2–3 times. Drizzle with balsamic vinegar. Garnish with lemon zest.

043

Brussels sprout

Full of plant compounds, B-vitamins, vitamin C, and fiber, Brussels sprouts help to keep us free from many conditions associated with aging.

NUTRIENTS

B-vitamins, vitamin C, folate; phytonutrients; fiber

Brussels sprouts are chock-full with phytonutrients, such as sulforaphane, which triggers the release of detoxifying and anti-carcinogenic enzymes. The vegetables are also rich in fiber, thus staving off digestive complaints. Brussels sprouts have lots of immunity-building vitamin C, which keeps us youthful by preventing eye disease and protecting the memory. They are also a source of folate, which fights heart disease.

BRUSSELS SPROUTS WITH BACON

1lb. Brussels sprouts, trimmed and washed
4oz. bacon strips, diced
¾ cup roasted, salted pistachios, shelled
¼ cup balsamic vinegar

Steam the Brussels sprouts 5–10 minutes, until almost tender. In a skillet cook the bacon until crisp. Remove, and add the Brussels sprouts to the pan; sauté 1–2 minutes. Add the pistachios and vinegar. Continue to cook 1–2 minutes, reducing the vinegar and glazing the sprouts and nuts. Add the bacon, season, mix well and serve.

044

Swiss chard

Rich in iron and other health-giving nutrients, Swiss chard is important for any anti-aging diet.

The iron in Swiss chard helps the body to produce red blood cells to transport oxygen. Swiss chard also contains vitamin C, which improves iron absorption in the body, as well as helping to eliminate toxic heavy metals and prevent hair loss. The high levels of B-vitamins and minerals such as magnesium, potassium, and calcium protect the heart, while its carotenoid content fights cell damage by free radicals.

NUTRIENTS
B-vitamins, vitamin C, carotenoids; calcium, iron, magnesium, potassium, selenium

---

CREAMED SWISS CHARD

1 tbsp. olive oil
1 medium onion, sliced
1lb. Swiss chard
1 tbsp. all-purpose flour
1 cup low-fat evaporated milk
  or half-and-half
2 tsp. grated Parmesan
pinch of ground nutmeg

In a heavy pan, heat the oil. Add the onion, and cook 5–6 minutes on a low heat. Chop the chard into ribbons, and add to the pan. Cover and cook a further 3–4 minutes. Sprinkle in the flour and add the milk, stirring constantly, until the sauce thickens. Add the Parmesan and the nutmeg. Mix well and serve.

bok choy

NUTRIENTS:
Vitamins A, C; calcium

The freshest bok choy has firm white stalks and dark green leaves.

Popular in Chinese cooking, bok choy has a light, sweet flavor and is high in vitamins A and C, and calcium.

A type of Chinese cabbage, bok choy is unique in that it's one of the few vegetables to contain high levels of vitamin A, which is especially useful for maintaining eye health. It's also rich in antioxidant vitamin C, helping to keep everything youthful from the immune system to the gums, and the heart to the skin. Bok choy contains plenty of calcium for bones and teeth. It's also low in sodium and in calories, thus is a good choice for weight control.

BABY BOK CHOY IN SZECHWAN SAUCE

8 baby bok choy, quartered
  lengthwise
2 tbsp. peanut oil
2 tsp. grated ginger root
½ tsp. red chili paste
1 tbsp. hoisin sauce

In a wok stir-fry the bok choy in the oil about 3 minutes. Add the ginger and stir-fry a further 2 minutes. Then, add the chilli paste and hoisin sauce, and stir-fry a further minute. Serve immediately.

carrot

With their very high levels of beta-carotene, carrots have powerful anti-aging properties.

Beta-carotene, which the body converts into vitamin A, is especially important for eye health. It's also of great benefit to the skin, and the immune and digestive systems. Along with alpha-carotene, it is anti-carcinogenic and helps to reduce the risk of heart disease. Carrots are also loaded with fiber and water, which cleanse the liver, boost detoxification, and plump out the skin to stave off wrinkles. The vitamin C and silica content of carrots is also valuable for keeping the skin youthful.

Because carrot tops leach out the carrots' nutrients, cut them off before storing.

NUTRIENTS
Vitamins C, K, alpha-carotene, beta-carotene, folate; calcium, iron, silica, zinc; fiber

BEAUTY JUICE
(for skin, hair, and nails)

4 cucumbers
4 parsnips
8–12 carrots, scrubbed, with tops removed
2 lemons, peeled
1 green bell pepper

Cut the cucumber and parsnip lengthwise and feed through a juicer, followed by the carrots, lemons, and green pepper. Pour into glasses and serve.

◉ ◉ ♥ ✚ ◐

pumpkin

NUTRIENTS
Vitamin C, carotenoids; fiber

Pumpkin has high levels of carotenoids and antioxidants to stave off premature aging.

Bright orange in color, pumpkins are high in carotenoids, including beta-carotene, which have anti-carcinogenic properties and prevent heart disease and eye problems. Beta-carotene also helps to protect against the harmful and aging effects of the sun. Pumpkin contains plenty of vitamin C, which boosts immunity and preserves the skin.

PUMPKIN, PARSNIP, AND CARROT SOUP

1 tbsp. extra virgin olive oil
1 tbsp. butter
1 onion, chopped
8oz. piece pumpkin, skinned
    and deseeded
2 large parsnips
2 large carrots
3¾ cups chicken or vegetable
    broth
1–2 tbsp. lemon juice

Chop the vegetables. Heat the oil and butter in a pan and fry the onion until soft. Add the pumpkin, parsnips, and carrots, and stir well. Cover, and cook gently 5 minutes. Add the stock. Bring to a boil, cover and simmer 30 minutes. Leave to cool, then blend until smooth. Reheat in the pan and add lemon juice to taste. Serve immediately.

048

Brazil nut

Brazil nuts are high in "good" fats and are full of selenium, which keeps us young and healthy.

Brazil nuts are about 70 percent fat. Half of this is oleic acid, the building block for the omega-9 fatty acids that are excellent for the skin and have anti-inflammatory properties. The rest is made up of omega-6 and omega-3 essential fatty acids, which promote healthy skin, glossy hair, and a good memory. The abundant levels of vitamin E and selenium provide a strong boost to the immune system, while selenium also activates glutathione, which destroys harmful free radicals.

NUTRIENTS
Vitamin E; calcium, magnesium, selenium; oleic acid, omega-3 and omega-6 fatty acids; fiber; protein

BRAZIL NUT PESTO

handful of flat leaf parsley, coarsely chopped
¾ cup Brazil nuts, roughly chopped
1½ tbsp. water
pinch of tarragon, chopped
1 garlic clove, crushed
⅛ tsp. grated lemon zest
3 tbsp. extra virgin olive oil
2 tbsp. grated Parmesan
salt and pepper to taste

Preheat the oven to 400°F. In a food processor process the parsley, Brazil nuts, water, tarragon, garlic, and lemon zest into a coarse paste. Add the olive oil and the Parmesan, and blend until smooth. Season and serve.

✳️almond

NUTRIENTS
B-vitamins, vitamin E, essential fatty acids; iron, magnesium, potassium, zinc; plant sterols; protein; fiber

Almonds contain a host of oils and nutrients that are especially good for keeping the skin youthful.

Almonds are a good source of protein, needed for healthy growth and the repair of cells. The nuts also contain more fiber than any other nut, thereby helping to maintain good digestion. Their calcium content helps to keep bones strong and to stave off osteoporosis. They also contain monounsaturated fats and plant sterols, which help to reduce the risk of heart disease.

To enhance the flavor of almonds, toast them in a pan over low heat until golden.

VITAMIN E FOR RADIANT SKIN

Almonds are a fantastic source of vitamin E, which plays an important role in maintaining healthy skin both internally and

ALMOND AND OATMEAL HOTCAKES

⅓ cup all-purpose flour
⅔ cup oatmeal
2 tsp. baking powder
⅓ cup finely ground almonds
1 egg
1 cup soy milk
cooking oil

Mix the flour, oatmeal, baking powder, and almonds together in a bowl. In a separate bowl, lightly beat the egg and soy milk and add to the dry ingredients; mix well. Put a splash of oil in a shallow pan, heat well, and add about ½ cup of the mixture. When golden and bubbles form on the upper side, turn and cook the other side. Repeat with the remaining mixture to make several hotcakes. Serve with bananas, honey, and yogurt.

externally, helping to preserve elasticity and repair damage. Almond oil, especially, is wonderfully soothing for the skin and effective in healing post-operative scars. Vitamin E also boosts immunity and protects the heart.

ABUNDANT MINERALS

Almonds provide zinc, magnesium, and potassium. While zinc strengthens immunity, magnesium increases energy and potassium reduces blood pressure, staving off heart disease.

TRADITIONAL ALMOND MILK *(to nourish the skin)*

⅔ cup finely ground almonds
2 tbsp. honey
2 cups still bottled water

In a bowl combine the almonds, honey, and water. Stir well, until the honey has dissolved. Leave 2 hours. Filter, and pour into a bottle with a lid. Apply generously to the face and neck with cotton wool, and leave on 20 minutes. Use in the morning and evening. Keeps 3 days in the refrigerator.

walnut

Walnuts are a wonderful snack food, providing many nutrients as well as a healthy oil.

Walnuts and walnut oil contain protein, vitamins B6 and E, potassium, magnesium, copper, and zinc, all of which help to keep us youthful. Vitamin B6 helps to prevent memory loss and protect the heart, while vitamin E maintains skin and hair. Both potassium and magnesium are good for the heart, and copper helps to prevent varicose veins. Zinc has a miraculous ability to rejuvenate the thymus gland and to boost immunity. Walnut oil is a good source of fatty acids, central to skin and heart health.

NUTRIENTS
B-vitamins, vitamin E; copper, magnesium, potassium, zinc; omega-3 fatty acids; protein

---

WALNUT, APPLE, AND CELERY STUFFING

6 tbsp. butter
1 large onion, minced
2 celery stalks, minced
2 cooking apples, chopped
6 cups fresh bread crumbs
2 cups chopped walnuts
½ tsp. dried thyme
1 large egg, beaten
½ cup milk

Preheat oven to 350°F. Gently heat the butter in a pan and cook the onion and celery . Mix the apples, bread crumbs, walnuts, and thyme in a bowl; stir in the vegetables, egg, and milk. Spoon into a baking dish. Bake 30 minutes. Serve.

cashew nut

Seeds of the Brazilian "cashew apple," cashew nuts are full of healthy fats and protein.

Cashew nuts are a great source of omega-6 essential fatty acids, which protect against heart disease. The nuts also contain magnesium, a nutrient that aids the function of the heart and enables the metabolism of calcium, which prevents osteoporosis. Rich in B-vitamins, which aid the maintenance of nerves and muscle tissue, and boost resistance to stress, cashews contain selenium to stave off wrinkles and promote glossy hair. They also provide iron to help to prevent anemia.

NUTRIENTS
B-vitamins, biotin, folate; iron, magnesium, manganese, potassium, selenium, zinc; omega-6 fatty acids; iodine; protein; fiber

CASHEW NUT CREAM

1 cup cashew nuts
½ cup soy milk
1 tsp. clear honey
½ cup sunflower oil
1 tsp. lemon juice

Put the cashew nuts and soy milk in a blender and blend until creamy. Add the honey, and slowly pour in the oil— you will notice the mixture thicken—then, add the lemon juice to set the cream. Chill before serving. Keeps in the refrigerator up to 5 days.

peanut

NUTRIENTS
Vitamin E, folate; potassium; arginine; fiber

Peanuts are full of heart-healthy nutrients and provide more protein than any other nuts.

Peanuts are high in monounsaturated fats, which reduce cholesterol levels and protect against clogged arteries and heart disease. The heart is protected further by the amino acid arginine, which the body converts to nitric oxide, helping to expand blood vessels and prevent clotting. Peanuts are also high in vitamin E, which maintains wrinkle-free skin and glossy hair. Because of their low glycemic index score, the nuts also help to prevent adult-onset diabetes.

SPICY CHICKEN SATAY

⅔ cup roasted peanuts, coarsely chopped
2 garlic cloves, crushed
½ tsp. ground ginger
1 tsp. curry powder
1 tsp. ground coriander
¼ cup soy sauce
2 tbsp. sesame oil
1 tbsp. brown sugar
pinch of chili powder
3 chicken breasts, skinless, chunked and put on skewers

In a skillet cook the peanuts, garlic, and ginger 2 minutes, then add all the other ingredients except the chicken. Leave to marinate overnight. Preheat the oven to 325°F. Place the skewers of chicken in a dish. Pour the marinade over and bake 10 minutes.

sesame seed

These tiny, nutrient-rich seeds were a symbol of immortality in ancient India.

Youth-enhancing sesame seeds and their oil are good sources of vitamin E, plus omega-6 and monounsaturated fats, which help to minimize heart disease and maintain healthy skin and hair. They also contain B-vitamins to support the nervous system and to help the body to cope with stress. The seeds and oil are an excellent source of calcium and magnesium, which are necessary for bone and heart health. They are rich in zinc to boost immunity, as well as selenium to stave off wrinkles.

NUTRIENTS
B-vitamins, vitamin E. calcium, iron, magnesium, zinc; omega-6 and omega-9 fatty acids

SESAME TAHINI DIP

1¼ cups sesame seeds
4 tbsp. peanut oil

Preheat the oven to 350°F. Sprinkle the sesame seeds on to a baking sheet and toast in the oven 20 minutes. Whizz the seeds in a blender about 3 minutes, then add 1 tablespoonful of oil and whizz 30 seconds before adding the remaining oil. Whizz again until a smooth paste is formed. Serve with a selection of roasted vegetable pieces.

sunflower seed

Although small, sunflower seeds are powerhouses of youth-enhancing antioxidant nutrients.

NUTRIENTS
B-vitamins, vitamin E; calcium, copper, magnesium, manganese, selenium, zinc; omega-6 fatty acids; protein

Sunflower seeds and oil are full of vitamin E, omega-6 essential fatty acids and monounsaturated fats, which help to keep the skin elastic and minimize heart disease. Omega-6 also helps to fight inflammation, thus relieving arthritis. The seeds and oil are rich in calcium and magnesium, needed for the contraction of muscles as well as a healthy bone structure. Magnesium is also used in producing energy. Sunflower seeds and oil also contain immunity-boosting zinc and selenium.

SUNFLOWER SEED OAT BREAD *(makes 2 small loaves)*

4½ cups oat flour
1 envelope (¼oz.) rapid-rise
   dry yeast
2 tbsp. sunflower seeds
1 tsp. salt
2 tbsp. malt extract
1⅔ cups warm water
1 tbsp. sunflower oil

Preheat the oven to 350°F. Put the flour, yeast, seeds, salt, and malt extract in a bowl; mix well. Add the water and oil. Form a dough. Knead 10 minutes; divide into 2 and place in loaf pans. Cover and leave 30 minutes. Bake 50–60 minutes until browned.

pumpkin seed

Tasty and nutritious, pumpkin seeds are full of essential fatty acids and micronutrients.

The abundant essential fatty acids found in pumpkin seeds are vital for youthful skin and glossy hair. EFAs are also central to a healthy brain, to boosting immune function, and decreasing inflammation. Pumpkin seeds are particularly high in zinc, offering defence against infections and boosting fertility. Together, EFAs and zinc have been linked to reducing prostate problems. Pumpkin seeds also contain calcium and magnesium for healthy bones, nerves, and muscles.

NUTRIENTS
B-vitamins; calcium, magnesium, selenium, zinc; omega-3 and omega-6 fatty acids; protein

PUMPKIN SEED BRITTLE

⅛ cup sugar
¼ cup water
⅔ cup pumpkin seeds
1 tsp. extra virgin olive oil
pinch of salt

Toast the pumpkin seeds. Toss them in a bowl with the oil and a pinch of salt. Then, spread them evenly on a baking sheet in the middle of a preheated oven at 250°F 1 hour; stir occasionally. In a skillet, combine the sugar and water, stirring constantly over low heat, until a deep caramel color. Add the pumpkin seeds, and stir until well coated. Tip out evenly on to a greased sheet of foil. Let cool completely and break into pieces to serve.

flax seed

NUTRIENTS
Calcium, magnesium, zinc; omega-3 and omega-6 fatty acids; lignans

With a sweet, nutty taste, flax seeds are loaded with essential fats for a youthful body and brain.

Flax seeds and flax seed oil are full of omega-3 and omega-6 essential fatty acids, which are central to youthful-looking skin and hair, an alert mind, a healthy heart, and an efficient immune system. The seeds and the oil also contain lignans, which have anti-carcenogenic properties. In addition, they provide calcium and magnesium for healthy bones.

> To make flax seeds more digestible, soak them in water for a few hours before eating them.

FLAX SEED FACE MASK
(to smoothe wrinkles)

**2 tsp. flax seeds
water, enough to cover
1 drop neroli oil**

In a small bowl, combine the flax seeds and water. Leave to stand until the seeds swell and the water turns to gel, then add the neroli oil. Using your fingers, spread the gel over your face and neck. Leave to dry, then rinse off with cool or tepid water. Pat your face dry.

oats

Oats are very versatile and are useful for preventing heart disease and boosting immunity.

As well as being a good source of energy-giving carbohydrates, oats are high in fiber, therefore maintaining steady blood sugar levels and preventing diabetes, and lowering cholesterol. They contain powerful, youth-promoting antioxidants, including vitamin E, tocotrienol, ferulic acid, and caffeic acid to fight against free radicals and protect against everything from heart disease to obesity and eye disease. Used topically, oats have a soothing, anti-inflammatory effect on the skin.

NUTRIENTS
B-vitamins, vitamin E, folate; iron, magnesium, selenium, silica, zinc; saponins; tocotrienol, ferulic acid, caffeic acid; protein; fiber

OATMEAL HERBAL SCRUB
(to decongest the skin)

**3 tbsp. dried parsley, lemon
   balm or fennel seeds**
⅔ cup boiling water
1 tbsp. ground oatmeal
2 drops almond oil

Make a herbal infusion by pouring the water over the herbs and covering for 15 minutes. Strain and discard the herbs. Allow the infusion to cool, then add enough to the oatmeal to form a paste-like consistency. Add the almond oil. Smooth the scrub on the face and neck and leave 20 minutes. Then, rinse off with tepid water and pat dry.

⊙ ⊘ ⊜ ⊚ ⊚ ♡ ♥

barley

NUTRIENTS
B-vitamins, vitamin E; selenium; tocotrienol; lignans; fiber

A great grain for the heart, barley is also full of antioxidants to fight damaging free radicals and the effects of aging.

Barley is the oldest cultivated cereal, and it was used widely by the Romans as a strengthening food. Today, it is largely neglected, but it has amazing nutritional properties.

BARLEY LOTION
(to improve blood circulation)

⅔ cup pearl barley
4 cups water
generous handful of fresh
   rosemary or 3 tbsp. dried
   rosemary

Cover the barley with cold water and soak 24 hours. Drain, and put the barley in a pan with the fresh water. Bring to a boil, cover and simmer 30 minutes. Strain and discard the barley. Add the rosemary to the barley water, cover and leave to infuse until cool. Strain into a secure glass bottle. Using cotton wool, apply twice daily. Store in the refrigerator up to 4 days.

A HEALTHY HEART

Barley is one of the richest sources of the antioxidant tocotrienol, which studies have shown to be even more potent than some forms of vitamin E in preventing heart disease. It works in two ways. First, they help to stop free radical oxidation, a process that makes "bad" cholesterol more likely to stick to artery walls. And second, they act on the liver to reduce cholesterol production. The grain also contains lignans that help to prevent tiny blood clots from forming, further reducing the risk of heart disease.

VALUABLE NUTRIENTS

Barley is exceptionally high in both selenium and vitamin E, which together have anti-carcinogenic properties. Vitamin E plays a pivotal role in keeping the skin and hair healthy and young-looking, while selenium is efective in fighting viral infections, protecting the heart from muscle damage and the eyes from disease.

Barley also contains calcium, potassium, and B-vitamins, which help to keep the bones strong, blood pressure in check, and the nervous system and the brain healthy. In addition, barley is full of soluble fiber, which aids digestion.

Pot barley is better than pearl barley, as it retains much more fiber.

whole wheat

NUTRIENTS
Vitamins B6, E; magnesium, zinc; pyroxidine; protein; fiber

A staple food in the Western diet, wheat is protein-rich, providing B-vitamins and minerals.

Whole wheat is a nutritious and healthy cereal grain. A valuable source of protein, it provides the building blocks for youthful skin, hair, and nails. It also provides a valuable source of energy, thus combating fatigue. Whole wheat is rich in B-vitamins, including B6, which maintains the nerves, prevents adult-onset diabetes, and also enhances the ability to register, retain, and retrieve information. The grain is a good source of zinc, which boosts immunity and aids eye health.

SIMPLE WHOLE WHEAT PIZZA CRUST

4¾ cups whole wheat flour
2 tbsp. active dry yeast
1½ tsp. salt
2 cups warm water
2 tbsp. extra virgin olive oil
2 tsp. honey
topping of choice

Preheat the oven to 400°F. Combine the flour, yeast, and salt in a bowl. Add the water, oil, and honey; mix well. Cover with a moist cloth and leave to rise in a warm place 10 minutes. Knead and press into a greased large pizza pan. Add the topping. Then, bake 15–20 minutes.

brown rice

Brown rice is an excellent source of fiber, as well as many valuable youth-preserving nutrients.

Fiber-rich brown rice keeps the digestive system in good health and helps to lower cholesterol in the blood. It's very high in B-vitamins, which are needed for a healthy brain and nervous system. Brown rice is also a source of magnesium, easing hypertension and helping the body to turn food into energy and prevent muscle cramps. Containing iron to combat anemia and premature hair loss, brown rice is also high in zinc, which promotes good immunity and healthy eyes. It is also said to boost sexual vigour.

NUTRIENTS
B-vitamins, folate; copper, iron, magnesium, manganese, zinc; protein; fiber

BROWN RICE PUDDING

4 cups water
1½ cups brown short-grain rice
2½ cups soy milk
4 tbsp. rice or date syrup
1 tsp. ground cinnamon
¼ nutmeg, grated
4 whole cloves
2 small handfuls of raisins
4 shavings of orange zest

Preheat the oven to 350°F. Put the water in a pan; bring to a boil. Add the rice and simmer 15 minutes. Strain and return the rice to the pan. Add the remaining ingredients and simmer 20 minutes. Spoon into a lightly greased dish. Bake 40 minutes.

millet

Extremely easy to digest, millet is particularly high in silica, which helps to keep the skin youthful.

NUTRIENTS
Magnesium, potassium, silica; protein

A fantastic source of silica, millet is a central ingredient in collagen, the body's "glue," which is needed for healthy hair, skin, teeth, eyes, nails, tendons, and bones. Silica also prevents cardiovascular disease and plays an important role in memory function. Besides being easily digestible, millet is the only alkaline-forming grain, thus helping to counteract over-acidity in the stomach and joints. It is also protein-rich, containing all eight essential amino acids that aid recovery after illness.

MILLET PILAFF

1 large onion, minced
4 tsp. extra virgin olive oil
2 tbsp. ground coriander seeds
2 garlic cloves, crushed
2 cups millet
1¼lb. tomatoes
2½ cups vegetable broth
1 cup white wine
2 tbsp. almonds, sliced
4–5 dashes of soy sauce

Preheat the oven to 350°F. Gently fry the onion in oil 4–5 minutes. Add the coriander and garlic; fry 5 minutes. Add the millet and cook 2 minutes. Add the tomatoes, broth, and wine. Boil, then simmer uncovered 20 minutes, until tender. Add the almonds and soy sauce. Serve immediately.

quinoa

Quinoa provides a spectrum of B-vitamins for health and youthfulness.

A complete protein, quinoa helps tissue to grow and also repairs it. Quinoa contains several B-vitamins, including B5, which is essential for a healthy response to stress. Full of iron, it is a high-energy grain, thus preventing fatigue, as well as hair loss and anemia. It also supplies the body with magnesium, which is well-known for preventing hypertension, and vitamin B2, which controls cholesterol build-up by destroying harmful free radicals. Quinoa also contains vitamin E, which is good for the skin.

NUTRIENTS

B-vitamins, vitamin E; calcium, iron, magnesium, zinc; saponins; protein; fiber

QUINOA TABBOULEH

1 cup quinoa
1⅔ cups vegetable broth
2 tbsp. pine nuts, toasted
8 cherry tomatoes, diced
2 onions, minced
1 tbsp. each finely chopped
    parsley, mint, and cilantro
4 tbsp. fresh lemon juice
2 tbsp. extra virgin olive oil

Rinse and drain the quinoa, then put in a pan. Toast 3 minutes. Add the broth and bring to a boil. Reduce heat, cover and simmer 12 minutes. Drain and put in a bowl. Add the pine nuts, tomatoes, onions, and herbs. In a dish combine the lemon juice and olive oil, and pour over the salad. Mix well and serve.

buckwheat

Buckwheat is high in rutin, a substance that strengthens tiny blood vessels.

Because of its rutin content, buckwheat is associated with circulatory health—it strengthens blood capillaries, thus preventing the formation of thread veins. Buckwheat contains fiber and all eight essential amino acids, and is a good source of protein for the brain. Rich in magnesium, the grain contains B-vitamins, which help to maintain the nervous system. It also lowers blood cholesterol levels.

NUTRIENTS
B-vitamins, magnesium, rutin; protein; fiber

BUCKWHEAT MUESLI

1 cup buckwheat flakes
1 cup oats
1 cup sunflower seeds
¼ cup dried apricots
⅓ cup raisins

Chop the apricots into bite-size pieces. In a large mixing bowl, combine the ingredients thoroughly. The muesli keeps well in a sealed plastic container. Serve with regular milk or soy milk.

lentil

A staple food in many countries, lentils are one of the single most nutritious and digestible foods.

Whether red, green, or brown, lentils are a great source of protein, which we need to keep our skin, hair, teeth, and nails strong and healthy. Lentils also contain high levels of B-vitamins, particularly B3, which protects against poor memory, and B12, which helps to prevent everything from arthritis to tinnitus. Lentils are rich in iron, thus preventing anemia. They are also full of fiber and help to regulate digestion.

NUTRIENTS
B-vitamins, folate; calcium, iron, potassium, selenium, zinc; protein; fiber

LENTIL AND CUMIN SOUP

2 onions, chopped
4 garlic cloves, crushed
4 tsp. cumin seeds
3 tbsp. vegetable oil
1 bay leaf
½ tsp. dried oregano
12 cups chicken broth
3 cups drained canned green
  or brown lentils

In a pan sauté the onion, garlic, and cumin seeds in the oil. Add the bay leaf, oregano, and broth. Bring to a boil and simmer 10 minutes. Add the lentils and cook a further 10 minutes. Remove the bay leaf and purée the soup in a food processor. Serve garnished with sour cream and toasted cumin seeds.

soybean

NUTRIENTS
B-vitamins, vitamin E, folate; calcium, magnesium, manganese, potassium, zinc; phytic acid; saponins, isoflavones

SCRAMBLED TOFU

2 garlic cloves, crushed
½ large red bell pepper, diced
2 tbsp. extra virgin olive oil
10½oz. firm tofu
½ tsp. turmeric
½ tsp. salt
pinch of black pepper
1 medium onion, chopped
1½ tsp. soy sauce

In a skillet sauté the garlic and pepper in the olive oil 2 minutes. Crumble the tofu and add to the pan, then add the turmeric, salt, pepper, onion, and soy sauce. Cook 3 minutes, stirring occasionally. Remove from the heat. Serve with salsa and corn tortillas.

Eating a diet rich in soybeans is believed to help to prevent heart disease, as well as to promote youthfulness and longevity.

This versatile legume is central to the diet of the Japanese, who have the longest life spans in the world. In Western countries, soya is best known in its derivative forms—as tofu, soy milk, soy yogurt, soy sauce and as meat analogues, for example textured vegetable protein (TVP).

FIGHTING DEGENERATIVE DISEASES

Soybeans are an excellent source of plant protein, dietary fiber, and complex carbohydrates. They are known to have a cholesterol-lowering effect and to prevent high triglyceride levels, which can cause heart disease. In addition, soybeans contain youth-preserving antioxidants, such as phytic acid, which can help to prevent clogging of the arteries.

However, perhaps the most useful attribute of soybeans is that they are extremely rich in micronutrients, such as saponins and isoflavones. A type of flavonoid, isoflavones are converted by the body into phytoestrogens and have anti-carcinogenic properties as well as the ability to promote bone health and reduce the risk of cardiovascular disease.

The beans contain vitamin E, which is vital for preserving youthful skin and hair, and B-vitamins, which maintain the nervous system and keep stress from causing premature aging. The beans also have an extremely low glycemic index score, thus helping to prevent diabetes and alleviating various menopausal symptoms.

When buying soy products, it is worth taking the time to check that they are free from GM soy.

garbanzo

Garbanzos have a unique savory, nutty flavor and are rich in many youth-preserving nutrients.

NUTRIENTS
B-vitamins, vitamin E, folate; iron, potassium, zinc; protein; fiber

Also known as chickpeas, garbanzos are a good source of protein, which is vital for the healthy repair of cells. Their high vitamin E content boosts the immune system, protects the heart, and promotes healthy skin and hair. They also contain zinc, which enhances immunity and rejuvenates the thymus gland. In addition, garbanzos are a useful source of isoflavones, which mimic estrogen and have anti-carcenogenic properties.

BAKED CHILI GARBANZOS

3 onions, sliced
1 fresh chili, minced
⅔ cup extra virgin olive oil
4 garlic cloves
2 tbsp. dried oregano
19-oz. can garbanzos, drained

Preheat the oven to 300°F. Sauté the onions and chili in the oil until soft, then add the garlic, oregano, and garbanzos. Mix well and transfer to a casserole. Add enough water to cover the garbanzos, cover with a lid and bake 1–1½ hours or until tender. Add a little more water during cooking if needed.

067

kidney bean

Kidney beans are high in protein, fiber, and nutrients that maintain health and well-being.

Popular in Central and South America, kidney beans are an excellent source of protein, which helps to keep energy levels steady as well as maintaining cells. They are also rich in folate, which is good for healing wounds, and to help prevent heart disease. Kidney beans are full of fiber, which is vital for keeping cholesterol levels down and aiding digestion. They are also a valuable source of iron, helping to prevent anemia.

NUTRIENTS
Folate; iron, manganese, potassium, protein, fiber

KIDNEY BEAN GUMBO

1 red onion, chopped
1 red bell pepper, deseeded
  and diced
1 celery stalk, chopped
2 garlic cloves, crushed
1 tbsp. olive oil
6 cups vegetable broth
2½ cups diced tomatoes
1 tsp. dried thyme
pinch of cayenne pepper
1½ cups drained canned kidney
  beans

In a pan fry the onion, pepper, celery, and garlic in the oil 5 minutes. Add the broth, tomatoes, thyme, and cayenne; cover and simmer until soft. Add the kidney beans and simmer 10 minutes. Serve.

068

sardine

NUTRIENTS
B-vitamins; calcium, iron, phosphorus, potassium, selenium; omega-3 fatty acids; protein

Fresh and canned sardines contain a host of age-defying fatty acids and antioxidants.

Some of the most beneficial nutrients for keeping our skin looking young and radiant are omega-3 fatty acids, and sardines are an excellent source.

PROTECT THE SKIN

However, the benefits of omega-3 fats are more than skin-deep. Several studies show that they help to make the blood less liable to clot and so reduce the risk of heart disease. They also keep the eyes healthy. In addition, research suggests that they

---

BROILED SARDINES WITH SALSA VERDE

2 large onions, chopped
2 garlic cloves, peeled
2 large green bell peppers, deseeded and chopped
½ cup extra virgin olive oil
2oz. canned anchovies
2 small green chilis, deseeded
zest and juice of 2 lemons

2 tbsp. capers
8 tbsp. chopped basil
4 level tbsp. chopped parsley
12 fresh sardines, washed

In a pan gently heat the onion, garlic, and peppers with half the oil. Put in a food processor with

the anchovies, chilis, lemon zest and juice, capers, and herbs and whizz into a chunky purée. Broil the sardines on foil under a hot broiler 5–7 minutes on each side. Lay on a plate, drizzle over the salsa and serve.

may help to protect the skin against sun exposure and ultra-violet radiation.

ANTIOXIDANT-RICH

Sardines also provide selenium, a powerful antioxidant that helps to prevent wrinkles and heart disease. Selenium is anti-carcinogenic and neutralizes toxic metals in the body.

Canned sardines are a good source of calcium, which keeps bones strong and healthy.

salmon

NUTRIENTS
Vitamins A, B12, D; omega-3 fatty acids, dimethylaminoethenol, docosahexaenoic acid

Wild salmon is full of omega-3 fatty acids, which are renowned for their anti-aging properties.

Salmon is one of nature's best sources of omega-3 fatty acids as well as DHA (docosahexaenoic acid), both of which are renowned for reducing cardiovascular disease. They are also good for keeping the skin and hair youthful. Essential fatty acids have powerful anti-inflammatory properties, making them useful for arthritic conditions. DHA is especially important for the brain and the nervous system, helping to keep the memory working well.

WATERCRESS SALMON STEAKS

4 salmon steaks
4 tsp. extra virgin olive oil
juice of 1 lemon
bunch of watercress, washed and chopped
4 tbsp. mayonnaise
1 tsp. Tabasco sauce (optional)

Put the salmon steaks in a broiler pan. Drizzle 1 teaspoon of oil and lemon juice over each. Broil each side under medium heat 5 minutes. Put the watercress, mayonnaise, and remaining lemon juice in a blender and whizz until smooth. Season with salt, pepper, and Tabasco (if using). Spoon over the salmon and serve.

shrimp

Shrimp are an excellent source of B-vitamins and minerals with youth-enhancing attributes.

Shrimp are rich in vitamin B12, which promotes brain function and prevents fatigue, and vitamin B3, which is crucial for preserving the memory. Their selenium content is anti-carcinogenic and essential for heart health. Selenium also fights off wrinkles. Shrimp supply iodine, which is vital for the proper functioning of the thyroid gland, and calcium for strong bones. They are also rich in zinc, which boosts immunity and fertility.

NUTRIENTS
B-vitamins; calcium, iodine, magnesium, phosphorus, potassium, selenium, zinc; protein

SHRIMP PÂTÉ

1lb. shelled cooked shrimp
3 tbsp. butter
3 tbsp. cream cheese
1 tbsp. sour cream
2 drops Tabasco sauce
½ tsp. ground nutmeg
I garlic clove, crushed
1 tbsp. lemon juice
pinch of salt and pepper

Put the shrimp (reserving one) in a blender with all the other ingredients. Whizz until smooth. Place the pâté in a serving dish and garnish with the whole shrimp. Serve with hot toast triangles.

herring

NUTRIENTS

B-vitamins, vitamin, A, D, E; omega-3 essential fatty acids; protein

PICKLED HERRING

¾ cup water
¾ cup white vinegar
2 garlic cloves
¼ tsp. dill seeds
⅓ cup sugar
2lb. salt herring fillets
1 red onion, sliced into rings

In a pan bring the water, vinegar, seasonings, and sugar to a boil, stirring until the sugar dissolves. Leave to cool. Cut the herring into 1-inch pieces, removing the bones. In 2 large jars, arrange the herring and the onion rings in alternate layers. Cover with the pickling solution. Chill at least 3 days before serving. Store up to 3 weeks.

With up to 20 percent of their weight being made up of essential fatty acids, herring are an important anti-aging food.

High in omega-3 fats, herring has extremely powerful anti-inflammatory properties, thus preventing and relieving arthritic conditions, reducing the risk of cardiovascular disease, and protecting the memory. Herring is high in zinc, which boosts the immune system. It is a protein-rich food and also contains many vitamins—the fat-soluble vitamins A, D, and E, as well as the water-soluble B-vitamins.

When buying kippers (smoked herring), choose undyed fish to avoid added chemicals.

072

haddock

A member of the cod family, haddock contains many nutrients to help us stay younger and fitter.

Haddock contains several B-vitamins to boost brain power and fight fatigue. It's especially high in folate, which helps to protect against heart disease, diabetes, and osteoporosis by reducing the body's levels of homocysteine. Folate may also have anti-carcinogenic properties. Haddock is an excellent source of iodine, which is needed to produce thyroid hormones that regulate the body's metabolism. The fish also contains zinc for immunity, sulphur to beautify the skin, and calcium to boost bone health and help to prevent conditions such as osteoporosis.

NUTRIENTS
B-vitamins, folate; calcium, iodine, sulphur, zinc; essential fatty acids; protein

BEER BATTERED HADDOCK

**1 cup all-purpose flour
pinch of salt and pepper
1 bottle (9fl. oz.) beer
2lb. fresh haddock**

In a bowl combine the flour, salt, pepper, and beer. Cut the haddock into pieces and dip into the batter. Then put them directly in a pan of hot oil. Cook on a low to medium heat 5 minutes on each side or until golden.

oyster

NUTRIENTS
Vitamins B3, B12, D, E; calcium, iron, magnesium, selenium, zinc

A renowned aphrodisiac, oysters are packed with health-boosting vitamins and minerals.

Oysters contain vitamins B3 and B12, which are useful to prevent memory problems. They are a valuable source of zinc, which helps to build resistance to disease, maintain youthful skin, and prevent hair loss. Oysters also contain vitamin E, which is also good for the skin and for preventing heart disease, as well as conditions such as arthritis. The shellfish are an excellent source of iron, which combats anemia. They provide vitamin D, as well, for healthy bones and teeth.

OYSTER BISQUE

1 qt. oysters, shelled
2½ cups vegetable broth
salt
white pepper
4 cups milk
1 cup light cream
1 tbsp. potato flour
a little butter

In a pan boil the oysters in the broth about 30 minutes. Strain, then add the salt, pepper, milk, and cream. Simmer gently 2 minutes. Mix the potato flour with the butter; add the mixture to the pan and stir well to thicken. Serve immediately.

lamb

Lean lamb is an excellent source of protein and easily absorbed iron.

NUTRIENTS
B-vitamins; iron, selenium, sulphur; protein

High in protein, which is necessary for the repair of aging cells, lamb is also a rich source of B-vitamins, including vitamin B12, which is vital for a healthy heart. The meat is also high in easily absorbed iron, which is fundamental for preventing anemia. The selenium in lamb protects the eyes from disease and the heart from muscle damage. Lamb is a source of sulphur, good for strong hair and nails.

Some lamb contains growth hormones, so always opt for organic, free-range lamb.

LAMB SHANKS IN TOMATO-ORANGE SAUCE

4 lamb shanks
2½ cups crushed tomatoes
1 cup water
1 tbsp. crushed garlic
grated zest and juice of 1 orange
2 tbsp. finely chopped fresh mint

Lightly oil a large pan. Add the lamb and cook, turning as needed, 10 minutes or until lightly browned on all sides. Add the tomatoes, water, garlic, orange zest, and juice to the pan. Cover and simmer 2–3 hours or until the meat is tender. Stir in the mint, and serve.

beef

Beef contains many nutrients, especially iron, which boosts the oxygen level in the blood.

A good source of protein, beef is also high in B-vitamins, including B12, which prevents fatigue and memory loss. It is rich in iron, which staves off conditions such as anemia and premature hair loss. Free-range, grass-fed beef is a good source of conjugated linoleic acid (CLA), a fatty acid shown to promote weight loss. Beef is also a source of sulphur, which our bodies need to maintain youthful hair and nails.

NUTRIENTS

Vitamin B12; iron, sulphur, zinc; conjugated linoleic acid; protein

---

BEEF STIR-FRY

4 tbsp. soy sauce
2 tbsp. dark roasted sesame oil
2lb. beef steak, cut into strips
4 garlic cloves
2 tbsp. minced fresh gingerroot
¼ tsp. chili flakes
2 red bell peppers, sliced

Combine the soy sauce and half the oil and pour over the beef. Heat the remaining oil, add the garlic, gingerroot, and chili flakes and cook 30 seconds. Stir-fry the pepper 2 minutes. Remove from the pan, add the beef and cook over a high heat 3–4 minutes. Add the vegetables and reheat.

chicken

Extremely popular and hugely versatile, chicken is bursting with health-giving nutrients.

Chicken is a good source of protein, contributing to the growth and repair of the body's cells, and, with the skin removed, is low in fat. It's rich in selenium, which helps to prevent wrinkles and keep the hair glossy. Chicken also contains iron and zinc to boost energy levels and immunity—there is twice as much in the dark meat as in the breast. The breast is particularly high in vitamin B6, which protects the heart.

NUTRIENTS
Vitamins B3, B6; iron, potassium, selenium, zinc; protein

SWEET AND SOUR CHICKEN DRUMSTICKS

8 chicken drumsticks, skinned
4 tbsp. clear honey
2 tbsp. sesame oil
6 tbsp. soy sauce
¼ cup lemon juice
4 tsp. coarsegrain mustard

Preheat the oven to 400°F. Put the drumsticks in a baking dish and pierce with a fork. Mix the honey, sesame oil, soy sauce, lemon juice, and mustard and pour over the chicken. Cook 25–30 minutes. Serve hot or cold.

0 🌀 🔆 👁 ♥ 👹 ✚

eggs

NUTRIENTS:
Vitamins A, B, D, E, lutein; selenium, zinc; lecithin, choline, zeaxanthin; protein

Eggs, both the whites and yolks, pack a powerful punch when it comes to anti-aging nutrients.

Protein-rich, eggs contain all eight essential amino acids, thus helping to make up the building blocks for the entire body—benefiting everything from skin to hair, and bones to muscles.

LOADED WITH VITAMINS

Eggs are also a wonderful source of zinc and vitamins A, B, D, and E. The zinc helps to boost immunity and is also vital for the production of collagen, which is needed for healthy, youthful skin. Vitamin A supports vision, vitamin D promotes strong bones, and vitamin E benefits the heart. Eggs are also a valuable source of selenium, which rejuvenates the immune system and protects the heart.

BRAIN FOOD

Owing to their high lecithin content, eggs are an important brain food, contributing not only to memory and concentration, but also to a healthy emotional state. Egg yolk is the richest known source of choline, which makes up cell membranes, helping the body to convert fats to acetylcholine, an important memory molecule in the brain.

EGG YOLK MASK
(to nourish dry skin)

1 tbsp. honey
1 large egg yolk
1 tsp. potato flour

In a bowl combine the honey, egg yolk, and potato flour, stirring to create a fine paste. Apply evenly to the face and neck and leave about 20 minutes. Rinse off with cotton wool and water. Pat dry. Repeat 2 or 3 times a week, making a fresh mask for each treatment.

CHOLESTEROL CONCERN

Many of us worry about the apparently high cholesterol content of eggs, but studies suggest this may be unfounded as the cholesterol in eggs doesn't circulate in the blood. In fact, of the 5g of fat contained in an egg, most is monounsaturated, which is the type that helps to lower the risk of heart disease.

Egg whites, as well as yolks, can be used in face masks, as they have great astringent qualities.

milk

NUTRIENTS: Vitamins B12, E; calcium, potassium

Best known for its calcium content, milk helps to strengthen the bones and fight off heart disease.

The abundance of calcium in milk gives it the ability to strengthen bones and to help to stave off osteoporosis. Studies have also shown that calcium may help to reduce blood pressure as well as cholesterol levels. Milk is a good source of vitamin B12, which combats memory and hearing problems, and fatigue. It also contains vitamin E, which benefits the eyes, skin, and immune system. Its potassium content is key in fighting heart disease. Skim milk is also believed to have anti-carcinogenic properties.

Even if you don't like to drink milk, you can add it to recipes to increase your intake.

MINT MILK BATH *(to nourish the skin and protect from aging)*

1 cup cornstarch
2 cups dried milk powder
4 tsp. crushed mint leaves
½ cup sea salt

Put all the ingredients in a jar and shake well to combine them. Add about 1 cup to running bath water. To obtain maximum benefit, soak in the bath 15 minutes.

bio-yogurt

Made by adding "friendly" bacteria to milk, bio-yogurt fights aging, both inside and out.

The live bacteria lactobacillus and bifidobacteria found in bio-yogurt help to maintain the correct level of acidity in the gut, and also enhance immunity. In addition, they lower cholesterol levels, reducing the risk of heart disease. Yogurt is rich in protein and calcium, which are essential for healthy bones and efficient muscles and nerves. Its vitamin B content boosts energy and protects the nervous system.

NUTRIENTS:
Vitamins A, B, C; calcium, iron, phosphorus, potassium, sodium; protein

BIO-YOGURT AND LEMON CLEANSER

**2 tsp. bio-yogurt
1 tbsp. lemon juice**

Mix the ingredients together in a small bowl. Apply to the face and neck area; leave 10 minutes. Rinse off with warm water and pat dry. (As well as acting as a cleansing agent, the bio-yogurt will have a cooling and refreshing action on your skin, while also rebalancing your skin's pH value. The yogurt's lactic acid content will brighten your skin, too.)

green tea

NUTRIENTS
Vitamins E, K; bioflavonoid antioxidants

Extremely high in bioflavonoids, green tea neutralizes the damaging effects of free radicals and fights premature aging.

Tea is the most popular beverage in the world, and green tea (comprising leaves that are lightly steamed when cut, rather than left to dry out like black tea) is fast becoming recognized for its youth-enhancing properties.

GREEN TEA AND PEACH REFRESHER

2 ripe peaches, pitted and
sliced
6 cups cold water
6 green tea teabags
honey, to taste
sprigs of mint

Put the peaches in a pan, add the water and bring to a boil. Put the teabags in a large pitcher and pour the water and peaches over them. Steep 6 minutes, then add the honey to taste. Leave to cool, then refrigerate until chilled. Pour the green tea and peach slices into glasses and garnish with mint to serve.

TREATS CONDITIONS

Green tea contains phenolic compounds that help to strengthen blood vessels, which makes it useful for treating conditions such as thread or varicose veins, as well as cold hands or feet. It also contains good amounts of vitamin E to help to boost immunity, promote healthy, glowing skin, and protect the eyes and the heart. The tannins in green tea offer further benefits for the eyes, as they act as an anti-inflammatory to relieve puffiness.

AMAZING ANTIOXIDANTS

The antioxidant bioflavonoids in green tea offer fantastic protection against heart and circulatory problems and have anti-carcinogenic properties. They also help to ward off wrinkles and preserve eye health. Bioflavonoids are said to rev up the metabolism and promote weight loss.

HEART HEALTHY

Green tea is also said to lower "bad" LDL cholesterol and triglyceride levels and raise "good" HDL cholesterol levels.

When making a cup of green tea, steep it for at least 3 minutes to gain its full benefits.

garlic

NUTRIENTS
Vitamin B6, C; calcium, sulphur; s-allylcysteine

Part of the onion family, garlic is famous for its anti-viral and heart-protecting properties.

Garlic contains a sulphur compound called allicin, which is released when garlic is crushed, encouraging the elimination of cholesterol from the body, lowering triglyceride levels, detoxifying the liver and acting as a potent anti-inflammatory. Its sulphur means that garlic helps in the formation of new cells, keeping the skin, nails, and hair young-looking. It is also said to help to treat cellulite. Garlic contains a compound, called s-allylcysteine, which appears to have an anti-carcinogenic action. Garlic is also a powerful immunity booster.

GARLIC BATH SOAK
(to soothe arthritis)

1 large fresh bulb garlic

Crush the garlic and add it to running bath water. Relax and soak in the bath for at least 15 minutes to gain the full anti-inflammatory benefits.

parsley

Parsley is full of youth-enhancing nutrients and is a natural healer.

NUTRIENTS
Vitamins A, B, C; calcium, copper, iron, magnesium, potassium

Parsley is the richest herbal source of the mineral potassium, which reduces hypertension—the number one cause of heart attacks. Potassium also stimulates the kidneys to eliminate waste matter. Parsley has anti-inflammatory properties, thus protecting against arthritis. It's also an excellent source of vitamin A for the eyes, and magnesium and calcium to protect the bones and the nervous system. The herb is rich in manganese, which boosts the memory, iron to prevent fatigue, and vitamin C for strong immunity.

Potassium is destroyed in cooking, so eat parsley raw to obtain maximum benefits.

FRESH PARSLEY MASK
(to tone and nourish the skin)

1 tbsp. chopped parsley
1 tbsp. honey
1 tbsp. fresh milk

In a bowl combine all the ingredients and mix into a thin paste. Apply to the face and leave 20 minutes. Rinse off with warm water and pat dry.

083

ginger

Ginger boosts the digestive system and has excellent anti-inflammatory properties.

NUTRIENTS
Vitamin B6; potassium, magnesium, copper, manganese; gingerol

Ginger protects the digestive system against premature aging, thus aiding the general absorption of nutrients. The root helps to regulate blood sugar, both by stimulating pancreas cells and by lowering cholesterol levels. Because ginger is such an effective anti-inflammatory, it is among the most respected herbs for the treatment of joint problems such as arthritis. Its main active constituent is gingerol, which has strong antioxidant properties. Ginger also boosts blood circulation.

GINGER BEER

2-liter bottle still water
1 cup sugar
plastic funnel
¼ tsp. active dry yeast
juice of 1 lemon
1½–2 tbsp. shredded
   gingerroot

Decant the bottled water into another container. Pour the sugar into the empty bottle through the funnel, then add the yeast. Mix the lemon juice with the ginger. Using the funnel, pour the mixture into the bottle. Add the water (leaving a 1-inch gap at the top). Shake well and leave in a warm place 24–48 hours, then store in the refrigerator overnight. Pour into glasses through a strainer. Serve.

turmeric

With its bright yellow color, turmeric offers a range of youth-enhancing benefits.

Turmeric is perhaps best known for its ability to relieve inflammatory conditions. It contains curcumin, a potent antioxidant, which is very effective at fighting free radicals and therefore protects the skin, eyes, and hair, and keeps them youthful. Curcumin also has anti-bacterial, anti-carcinogenic, and cholesterol-lowering properties. It is an anti-coagulant, therefore reducing the risk of heart attacks. Research shows that curcumin may also protect against memory deterioration.

NUTRIENTS
Vitamins A, C; curcumin; iron

Avoid exposure to the sun if taking turmeric medicinally, as it can increase sensitivity.

SEA BASS FILLETS WITH TURMERIC AND LIME RUB

1 tsp. salt
juice of 1 lime
1 tsp. ground turmeric
4 sea bass fillets
3 tbsp. vegetable oil

In a bowl, mix the salt, lime juice, and turmeric together. Rub into the sea bass fillets. Heat the oil in a non-stick skillet, add the coated fillets and cook 2–3 minutes on each side. Serve with a vegetable dhal.

fennel

NUTRIENTS
Vitamin C, folate; potassium;
phytonutrients; fiber

Especially popular in French and Italian cuisine,
fennel boasts a host of anti-aging properties.

Rich in phytonutrients, including rutin, quercetin, and
anethole—the primary components of its volatile oil—fennel
has been shown to reduce inflammatory conditions such as
arthritis. It is also an excellent source of vitamin C, which is
needed for the proper functioning of the immune system, to
protect the brain, and to avoid aging of the arteries. Fennel
is fiber-rich and may help to reduce elevated
cholesterol levels. In addition, it's a good source of
folate, which lowers the risk of heart disease.

FENNEL SEED INFUSION (to cleanse and tone the skin)

2 tsp. fennel seeds, crushed
2 sprigs fresh thyme, crumbled,
  or ½ tsp. dried thyme
½ cup boiling water
juice of ½ lemon

In a bowl, combine the fennel
seeds and thyme, and cover with
the boiling water. Add the lemon
juice and steep 15 minutes.
Strain, and when cold, store,
covered, in a jar in the
refrigerator. Dab evenly on the
face and neck every morning
with cotton wool, then rinse off
with warm water.

086

⬤ ◉ ♥ ⚇ ✚ ◔

dandelion

Dandelion aids detoxification, thus keeping the body free of age-accelerating toxins.

With its detoxifying action dandelion is useful for treating water retention, promoting weight loss, and boosting energy. It's also a good source of beta-carotene and lutein, which have anti-carcinogenic properties. Dandelion contains vital nutrients including vitamins A, B, and C. Vitamin A keeps the eyes young and healthy, while B-vitamins maintain the nervous system and the brain. Vitamin C is key to immune function and also protects the heart. Dandelion is high in calcium for the bones, and copper, which helps to prevent varicose veins.

NUTRIENTS
Vitamin A, B, C, D; calcium, copper, iron, potassium

DANDELION AND MANDARIN SALAD

3 tbsp. extra virgin olive oil
3 tsp. cider vinegar or lemon juice
about 2 cups (5oz.) dandelion leaves
¾ cup sliced scallions
6 hard-cooked eggs, sliced
1½ cups mandarin segments
dandelion flowers (optional)

Combine the oil and vinegar to make the dressing. In a salad bowl combine the dandelion leaves and scallions; add the dressing and toss to coat. Arrange on 4 plates; top with the eggs and mandarin segments. Garnish with the dandelion flowers if you like.

cayenne pepper

NUTRIENTS
Vitamins A, B, C; calcium, manganese, potassium; capsaicin; fiber

Hot and spicy, cayenne pepper is packed with nutrients to keep the symptoms of aging at bay.

Cayenne pepper is a rich source of vitamins A and C, as well as all the B-vitamins. It's therefore useful for everything from eye health to immune function, and healthy skin to good memory. Cayenne is also very high in calcium, which staves off osteoporosis, and potassium, which is good for the heart. The pepper has a high concentration of capsaicin, which has been widely studied for its pain-reducing effects, cardiovascular benefits, and ability to help to prevent ulcers. Capsaicin also gives cayenne its anti-inflammatory properties.

WARMING CAYENNE WAX
(to treat painful, inflamed joints)

8oz. beeswax
2 fresh cayenne peppers,
or 1 dried cayenne pepper
⅔ tsp. St.-John's-Wort

In a heavy pan melt the beeswax and add the cayenne pepper. Simmer 10 minutes, then remove the pepper. Stir in the St.-John's-Wort. Pour the warm mixture into empty ice cube trays and freeze. Melt 1 cube as needed. As it melts, lay out some tissue and, using a pastry brush, paint on the wax in a strip. Wrap the tissue strip around the painful area. To retain heat, cover the area in plastic wrap. Leave on 20 minutes. Repeat 3 times a week.

088

chamomile

Best known as a relaxant, chamomile is a popular remedy for insomnia and digestive complaints.

NUTRIENTS
Flavonoids; tannins

Chamomile relaxes the muscles throughout the body. Its bitters stimulate the flow of bile and the secretion of digestive juices, enhancing the appetite and improving sluggish digestion. The herb is very soothing and helps to induce relaxation and sleep. Used topically, chamomile treats inflamed joints and stiff muscles. It also has cosmetic benefits: when used in face creams, it promotes a youthful, glowing complexion. Chamomile is also known for being a powerful conditioner that leaves the hair softer and shinier.

CHAMOMILE HAIR TREATMENT

handful of chamomile flowers
⅓ cup olive oil

Combine the chamomile and oil in a jar with a lid. Stand on a sunny windowsill and shake at least once a day. After 2 weeks, strain and discard the chamomile. Brush out your hair and apply to the hair ends, avoiding the scalp, using about 2–4 teaspoonfuls, depending on the length of your hair. Leave on about 10 minutes, then shampoo as normal.

ginseng

The Chinese have revered ginseng for 5,000 years as an overall antidote to the ravages of aging.

Ginseng is a renowned performance enhancer, not just for physical work but for mental tasks, too. A great energizer, ginseng helps to combat fatigue and is also believed to fight heart disease, as well as combat impotence. Ginseng contains choline, a chemical vital to the brain for learning and memory retention. It also contains antioxidants to defy the effects of aging, and compounds with estrogenic properties, which relieve menopausal symptoms.

NUTRIENTS
Choline; saponins

SPICED GINSENG ICED TEA

8 cups water
8 cardamom pods, crushed
6 whole cloves
2 cinnamon sticks
1 star anise pod
8 ginseng teabags
¼ cup honey
ice cubes

In a large pan combine the water with the cardamom pods, cloves, cinnamon sticks, and star anise, and bring to a boil. Remove from the heat and add the teabags; leave them to steep 5 minutes. Remove the teabags and stir in the honey until dissolved. Strain the tea into a pitcher and leave to cool, then refrigerate until chilled. Serve in tall glasses over ice.

paprika

Commonly found in powdered form, paprika is a wonderful circulatory stimulant.

Paprika derives its bright, orange-red color from carotenoid pigments, which protect the body from free-radical damage. The spice also has a high concentration of capsaicin, recognized for its pain-reducing effects, as well as its cardiovascular benefits. Capsaicin's anti-inflammatory properties make paprika useful for the treatment of arthritis. Paprika also contains sizeable amounts of vitamin C, which is vital for youthful skin and a strong immune system.

NUTRIENTS
B-vitamins, Vitamin C, carotenoids; capsaicin; anthocyanins

BAKED COD WITH PAPRIKA

2 or 3 onions, sliced
1 tsp. paprika
¼ cup butter
3lb. cod fillets, skinned
juice of 1 lemon
salt and pepper
pinch of dried rosemary
½ cup sour cream

Preheat the oven to 375°F. Sauté the onions, with half the paprika in half the butter. Mix the lemon juice with water in a bowl and rinse the cod. Put in a baking dish with remaining butter. Season with salt, pepper, rosemary, and rest of paprika. Cover with onions and sour cream. Bake 30 minutes.

gingko biloba

NUTRIENTS
Flavonoids

GINGKO BILOBA AND ROSEMARY TONIC

handful of dried gingko leaves
handful of dried rosemary
enough vodka to cover

Place the gingko in a jar, cover with vodka and secure the lid. Repeat the process with the rosemary in a separate jar. Every few days shake the jars vigorously. After 4 weeks, strain the mixtures and discard the herbs. Combine the tinctures in 1 bottle. Put ½–1 teaspoonful of the tincture in a cup of hot water, stir and leave for a few minutes (this will allow most of the alcohol to evaporate). Take the tonic 2–3 times a day, preferably on an empty stomach.

An extract from the gingko leaf, gingko biloba has a remarkable ability to improve memory.

As we become older, our bodies typically produce fewer neurotransmitters, and our brain tends to be more forgetful and less alert. However, gingko biloba is said to increase the production of dopamine, which improves the brain's ability to transmit information. Research has also demonstrated that gingko improves the blood circulation, thus helping the brain and other organs to function efficiently. Gingko is rich in flavonoids, which are anti-carcinogenic and help to protect the body from heart disease and arthritis.

wheatgrass

Positively bursting with nutrients, wheatgrass is an elixir of youthfulness.

Wheatgrass contains all the vitamins except vitamin D. It's also rich in enzymes, minerals, and proteins. This makes it good for everything from the nervous system to the circulatory system, to eye health and skin elasticity. Wheatgrass is said to help to prevent tooth decay, and to stop hair going gray. Its high chlorophyll content boosts production of blood. Wheatgrass also helps to combat the toxins in the body, which left unchecked, can accelerate the aging process.

NUTRIENTS
Vitamin A, B-vitamins, vitamins C, E, K; calcium, magnesium, manganese, phosphorus, potassium, selenium, zinc; chlorophyll

GREEN GARDEN COCKTAIL

1 tray fresh wheatgrass
2 celery stalks
handful of parsley
masticating juicer

To harvest the wheatgrass, grasp a small bundle of blades firmly, and with a sharp knife, cut them off above the compost level. Rinse all the ingredients in cold water and feed them into a masticating juicer. Repeat with 2–3 more bundles of wheatgrass. Drink about 2 tablespoonsfuls each day on an empty stomach.

water

LEMON AND MINT WAKE-UP WATER

1 lemon
handful of mint leaves
2 cups water

Slice the lemon and place in a large pitcher. Carefully rub the mint leaves between the palms of your hands to bruise them slightly. Add them to the pitcher. Pour in the water, cover and chill overnight. In the morning strain the water mixture and discard the mint. Return the lemon slices to the water, pour into a large glass and sip.

Water is essential to our health and survival, and is well known for its revitalizing properties.

Water is central to our well-being. This is perhaps not surprising, given that the average adult is made up of about 70 percent water. However, most of us don't drink enough of it, and as a result, we live in a constant state of dehydration.

VITAL TO THE BODY

If our bodies don't have sufficient water, they can't eliminate waste products effectively, which causes problems such as kidney stones. Water is vital for the blood circulation and for chemical reactions in the digestive and metabolic processes. It carries nutrients and oxygen to cells through the blood, thus stimulating the organs. It also lubricates our joints, keeping us supple and agile. We need water for energy, and even to breathe—our lungs must be moist to take in oxygen. And, perhaps surprisingly, we also require plenty of water to avoid water retention and excess weight gain.

SKIN SAVIOR

Water also regulates and controls the natural pH balance of the skin—revitalizing, hydrating, oxygenating, and detoxifying it. Without water, the body is unable to rid itself of the harmful toxins that get trapped in the tissues, causing the complexion to deteriorate. Water is also needed to keep hair shiny and healthy.

WATER THERAPY
(to regulate the skin's natural pH balance)

A shower!

Adjust the water so that the temperature is comfortably hot, and shower 1 minute. Then, adjust the temperature to cold, and shower another minute. Repeat, alternating between hot and cold bursts another 5 minutes, or longer. Finish with a blast of cold water. Step out of the shower, wrap yourself in a warm towel and relax for a while before dressing.

094

alfalfa sprout

NUTRIENTS
Vitamin A, B-vitamins, vitamins C,
E; calcium, magnesium,
phosphorus, potassium, silica,
zinc; chlorophyll

Alfalfa sprouts are highly digestible and contain huge amounts of antioxidants.

These sprouted seeds provide abundant amounts of vitamin A for the eyes, B-vitamins for the nervous system and brain power, vitamin C for immunity and eye health, and vitamin E for the skin and the heart. They are also high in calcium and phosphorus for the bones, iron to prevent anemia, magnesium and potassium to lower the risk of heart disease, zinc to prevent premature hair loss, and silica to promote glowing skin, strong nails, and glossy hair.

SUNSHINE PITA POCKETS

1 cauliflower, steamed
¼ tsp. dry mustard
juice of ½ lemon
½ tsp. curry powder
tiny pinch of salt
¼ tsp. ground cardamom
⅓ cup mayonnaise
4 pita breads
4oz. alfalfa sprouts
3 carrots, grated
2 tomatoes, sliced

Mash the cauliflower in a bowl and mix in the mustard, lemon juice, curry powder, salt, cardamom, and mayonnaise. Chill in the refrigerator. Halve the pita breads, divide the mixture between them, then add the sprouts, carrots, and tomatoes.

wheat germ

The sprouting part of wheat grain, wheat germ is a super source of free-radical-fighting vitamin E.

Owing to its high vitamin E content, wheat germ is especially good for keeping hair glossy and skin glowing. It's also been shown to prevent heart disease. Wheat germ contains omega-6 fatty acids, thus relieving pain in the joints. Its choline content produces the neurotransmitter acetylcholine, which helps to boost memory. The brain also benefits from its B-vitamins. Used topically, wheat germ's slightly granular texture gently exfoliates sensitive or dry skin.

NUTRIENTS
B-vitamins, vitamin E; iron, magnesium, manganese, selenium, zinc; omega-6 fatty acids; choline; fiber

WHEAT GERM EXFOLIATING LOTION

1 cup milk
1 cup dried chamomile
4 tbsp. honey
8 tsp. wheat germ

Pour the milk into a cup and add the chamomile. Leave to infuse a few hours. Strain the liquid and discard the chamomile. Add the honey and wheat germ, and mix well. Pour the lotion into a bottle and store in the refrigerator up to a week. Apply to the face and neck, then rinse off with warm water. Use as needed.

brewers yeast

NUTRIENTS
B-vitamins; magnesium, zinc; lecithin, lipoic acid; protein

Brewers yeast is especially useful to boost energy levels and brain power.

Comprising almost 50 percent protein, as well as some lecithin and unrivalled levels of B-vitamins, brewers yeast is a valuable remedy for fatigue and lapses of memory. It's also rich in lipoic acid, which helps to keep the brain young and active. Brewers yeast is a good source of zinc to boost the immune system, as well as magnesium to promote a healthy heart. Used topically it is very effective for treating dry skin complaints. Holding up to 70 per cent moisture, it provides the building blocks for regenerating soft, supple, and healthy tissue.

BREWERS YEAST FACE PACK

1 tsp. crushed fennel seeds
½ cup water
1 tbsp. brewers yeast

In a small pan, simmer the fennel seeds in the water 10 minutes, then strain. Allow the infusion to cool to room temperature, then mix in the brewers yeast. Spread the mixture over the face and neck, and leave 10 minutes. Rinse off gently with warm water and pat dry.

cider vinegar

Made from fermented apple juice, cider vinegar is well known for its anti-arthritic properties.

The malic acid content of apple cider vinegar helps to dissolve calcium deposits in the body and eases arthritis. It also helps to balance the body's acid-alkaline pH levels and oxygenates the blood, thus aiding digestion and boosting the immune system. Enzyme-rich, cider vinegar contains the perfect balance of 19 minerals, as well as apple pectin, the water-soluble dietary fiber that binds to toxins in the body and assists in their removal, thus improving skin tone. Pectin also lowers cholesterol levels, and so helps to stave off heart disease.

NUTRIENTS
Iron, calcium, chlorine, fluorine, magnesium, potassium, phosphorus, silica, sodium, sulphur; malic acid; fiber

Apple cider vinegar is available as a fiber supplement, and is said to help with weight loss.

CIDER VINEGAR HAIR RINSE (to restore dull, lifeless hair)

1–2 tbsp. apple cider vinegar
3 cups water

Mix the cider vinegar and water in a pitcher. After washing and conditioning your hair as usual, pour the cider vinegar mixture over your hair as a final rinse.

honey

Best known as an energy food, honey also has many anti-aging properties.

Widely used as a natural sweetener, honey is composed of 79 percent sugar. The rest comprises water and small amounts of vitamins, including vitamin B6, which is good for the brain, and many minerals, including calcium to strengthen the bones. Honey also contains phytonutrients such as propolis, which helps to boost immunity, and caffeic acid, which has anti-carcinogenic properties. Used topically, honey is a humectant, attracting and retaining water, which keeps the skin soft and supple.

NUTRIENTS

B-vitamins; calcium, copper, iron, magnesium, manganese, phosphorus, potassium, sodium, zinc

FIRMING FACE MASK

1 tbsp. honey
1 egg white
1 tsp. glycerin
about ¼ cup all-purpose flour

In a small bowl, mix the honey, egg white, and glycerin. Then, add enough flour to form a paste. Smooth the mask over the face and throat. Leave 10 minutes, then rinse off gently with warm water.

coconut oil

Coconut oil is a unique source of medium-chain fatty acids—a great aid to staying youthful.

Coconut oil is extremely rich in medium-chain fatty acids (MCFAs), which are soluble and a great energy source, similar to carbohydrates. MCFAs have been shown to assist the absorption of calcium, magnesium, and some amino acids, as well as supporting the healthy function of the thyroid. MCFAs, particularly lauric acid, are great immunity boosters. They also stimulate metabolism, benefit the heart and promote weight loss. Rich in vitamin E, coconut oil keeps the skin's connective tissues strong and supple, which helps to prevent wrinkles.

NUTRIENTS
Vitamin E; medium-chain fatty acids

COCONUT BODY OIL

2½ fl. oz. tub coconut oil
15 drops of your favorite
**   essential oil**

Remove the lid from the coconut oil and place the tub in a large pan of water; heat gently, until the oil liquefies. Add your favorite essential oil and stir well. Replace the lid back and put the tub in the refrigerator 15 minutes. Apply generously all over your body (but not to your face). Beware that the oil could stain your clothes, so avoid dressing until the oil has soaked well into the skin.

olive oil

NUTRIENTS
Vitamin E; oleic acid; polyphenols; monounsaturated fats

A Mediterranean favorite, olive oil contains fats and antioxidants that are central to good health and youthful beauty.

Made from the crushing and the subsequent pressing of olives, olive oil contains vitamin E, which helps to keep skin wrinkle-free and hair glossy.

Always choose extra virgin olive oil, as this contains the optimum nutrients.

HOT OIL TREATMENT
(to treat a dry scalp and hair)

½ cup olive oil
½ cup boiling water

Pour the olive oil and boiling water into a large glass bottle or a jar with a lid. Shake well until the oil is emulsified. When the mixture has cooled slightly, massage into the hair, taking care not to burn the scalp. Put a shower cap or plastic bag over your hair and wrap it in a hot towel that has been soaked in hot water, then wrung out. Leave about 30 minutes, then shampoo as usual.

GOOD FATS

Olive oil is also rich in monounsaturated fat, which is believed to have anti-carcinogenic properties, and help to lower hypertension and prevent diabetes.

HEART HEALTHY

Research into the effectiveness of olive oil against clogging of the arteries reveals that the olives' monounsaturated fats prevent the oxidation of cholesterol, and therefore stop it from sticking to artery walls and causing heart attacks. Further studies suggest that olive oil also contains hefty concentrations of antioxidants, including chlorophyll, carotenoids, and polyphenolic compounds—all of which not only fight age-accelerating free radicals, but also protect the olives' important vitamin E content. Their rich supply of polyphenols, known to have anti-inflammatory and anticoagulant actions, are also thought to help stave off conditions such as osteoporosis and arthritis.

BEAUTIFUL SKIN

Olive oil is high in oleic acid, an omega-9 fatty acid, which demonstrates anti-inflammatory properties to calm and soothe the skin.

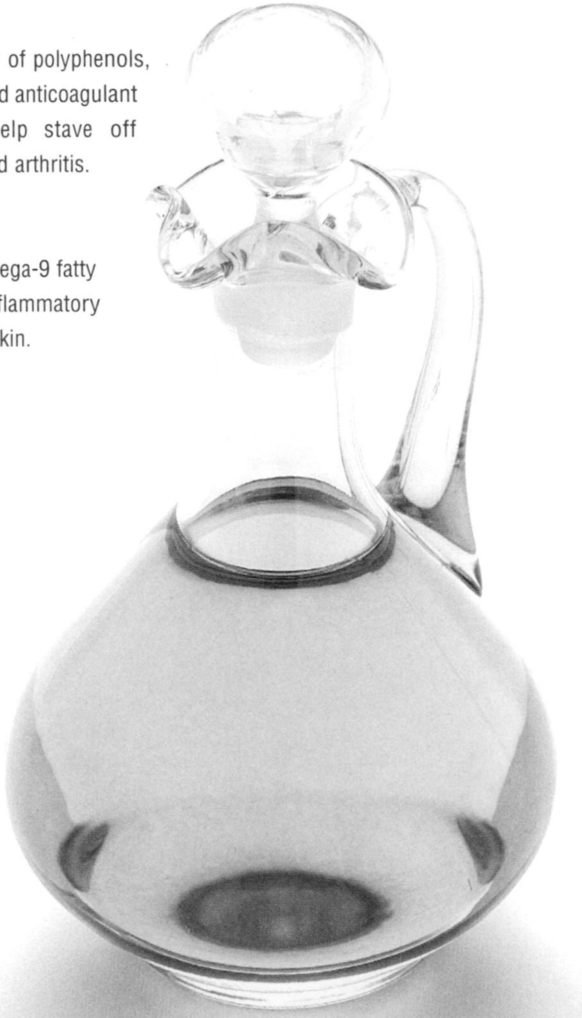

OLIVE OIL AND LEMON JUICE *(to soothe inflammation)*

2 tbsp. extra virgin olive oil
juice of ½ lemon

In a cup combine the olive oil and lemon juice. Mix well. Drink on an empty stomach every morning and wait at least 30 minutes before having breakfast. Repeat for at least 3 weeks to notice an improvement.

ailments directory

WRINKLES

We can get wrinkles at any age from our 20s onwards, depending on our life style and our genetic predisposition. Factors such as smoking, spending lots of time in the sun, and using sunbeds can all age the skin prematurely and exacerbate lines, particularly around the eyes. To fight wrinkles, reduce sun damage, and improve skin texture, eat foods full of vitamins A, C, and E and selenium.

Foods to eat:

Grape (p.10); Avocado (p.34); Onion (p.41); Radish (p.51); Almond (p.60); Cashew nut (p.63); Sesame seed (p.65); Chicken (p.91); Green tea (p.96)

LACKLUSTER HAIR

As we age, our hair follicles slowly become dormant—a natural process in both men and women. However, foods rich in iron and vitamin A nourish the hair follicles and can help to keep your hair looking thick and lustrous.

Foods to eat:

Prune (p.20); Spinach (p.45); Watercress (p.48); Swiss chard (p.55); Almond (p.60); Shrimp (p.85); Beef (p.90)

FATIGUE

If you feel tired all the time, you could well be anemic. This condition occurs when there is a decrease in the amount of oxygen-carrying hemoglobin found in your red blood cells. Symptoms include weakness, pale skin, and general fatigue. Eating foods rich in iron and vitamin B12 help to combat anemia at any stage in life.

Foods to eat:

Spinach (p.45); Almond (p.60); Cashew nut (p.63); Quinoa (p.75); Lentil (p.77); Kidney bean (p.81); Sardine (p.82); Lamb (p.89); Beef (p.90)

INSOMNIA

Sleep quality is a key factor in how you look and feel—good sleep makes you perform better both mentally and physically, and helps your eyes, skin, and hair to stay

healthy and bright. To get a good night's sleep, avoid stimulants such as coffee and chocolate for at least 5 hours before you go to bed, as they can interrupt sleep patterns or cause blood sugar highs and lows. Also, when snacking, eat foods containing natural sugars to keep your blood sugar levels stable.

Foods to eat:

Grape (p.10); Orange (p.16); Prune (p.20); Fig (p.30); Spinach (p.45); Sweet potato (p.50); Almond (p.60); Peanut (p.64); Pumpkin seed (p.67); Whole wheat (p.72); Quinoa (p.75); Lentil (p.77); Kidney bean (p.81); Haddock (p.87); Oyster (p.88); Chicken (p.91); Parsley (p.99); Ginger (p.100); Coconut oil (p.117)

DIGESTIVE COMPLAINTS

Digestive problems don't have to be an inevitable aspect of getting older. The key to keeping the digestive system in good shape is to eat plenty of fiber-rich foods and drink lots of water.

If you suffer from indigestion —discomfort, or a burning feeling in the oesophagus—try to reduce your intake of acid-forming foods, such as cheese and red meat, and eat more foods containing digestive enzymes and fiber.

Foods to eat:

Grape (p.10); Papaya (p.15); Banana (p.19); Black currant (p.22); Grapefruit (p.27); Watercress (p.48); Artichoke (p.49); Brussels sprout (p.54); Carrot (p.57); Almond (p.60); Whole wheat (p.72); Brown rice

(p.73); Millet (p.74); Buckwheat (p.76); Garbanzo (p.80); Bio-yogurt (p.95); Garlic (p.98); Ginger (p.100); Fennel (p.102); Dandelion (p.103); Cayenne pepper (p.104); Chamomile (p.105); Cider vinegar (p.115)

VARICOSE VEINS

Varicose veins are twisted, enlarged veins near the surface of the skin, which occur most commonly in the legs and ankles. Normally, the one-way valves in veins keep the blood flowing efficiently against gravity up toward the heart. However, when the valves fail to function properly, blood pools, pressure builds up and the veins become weakened. Vitamin C-rich foods, as well as those containing copper and phenolic compounds are

thought to help to prevent varicose veins.

Foods to eat:
Lemon (p.18); Walnut (p.62); Green tea (p.96); Fennel (p.102); Dandelion (p.103)

JOINT PROBLEMS

Keep your joints supple by eating antioxidant-rich fruits and vegetables, along with nuts, seeds, and oily fish. Some spices, such as cayenne pepper, may be used topically to help to relieve aching joints.

Foods to eat:
Apple (p.25); Pineapple (p.26); Cherry (p.32); Avocado (p.34); Sesame seed and oil (p.65); Sunflower seed and oil (p.66); Flax seed (p.68); Lentil (p.77); Salmon (p.84); Herring (p.86); Oyster (p.88); Parsley (p.99); Ginger (p.100); Turmeric

(p.101); Fennel (p.102); Cayenne pepper (p.104); Chamomile (p.105); Paprika (p.107); Ginkgo biloba (p.108); Wheat germ (p.113); Cider vinegar (p.115); Olive oil (p.118)

MEMORY LOSS

As we get older our bodies start to make less of the chemicals our brain cells need to work, thus making it harder to recall stored information. Studies have shown that vitamin E, magnesium, and other nutrients may help to counteract this and so prevent memory loss. Researchers are also studying the possibility that foods rich in antioxidants, particularly vitamins C and E and the mineral silica, might help to keep our brains fit and active in later life.

Foods to eat:
Mango (p.12); Fig (p.30); Beet (p.36); Bell pepper (p.39); Kale (p.43); Spinach (p.45); Cabbage (p.46); Watercress (p.48); Walnut (p.62); Sunflower seed (p.66); Pumpkin seed (p.67); Whole wheat (p.72); Millet (p.74); Salmon (p.84); Shrimp (p.85); Herring (p.86); Oyster (p.88); Egg (p.92); Parsley (p.99); Turmeric (p.101); Cayenne pepper (p.104); Ginseng (p.106); Ginkgo biloba (p.108); Wheat germ (p.113); Olive oil (p.118)

EYE DISEASE

If you want to keep your eyes shiny and bright, remember the old adage about eating your carrots—or, in fact, any brightly colored fruit and

vegetables. Studies suggest that the antioxidants they contain—including vitamins A, C, and E and lutein—benefit the eyes by helping the lenses to adjust to changes in light; maintaining the macula (the part of the eye that enables clear vision); and keeping the eyes moist.

Foods to eat:

Apricot (p.13); Blueberry (p.14); Pomegranate (p.31), Cherry (p.32); Beet (p.36); Bell pepper (p.39); Kale (p.43); Pumpkin (p.58); Swiss chard (p.55); Carrot (p.57); Sesame seed (p.65); Barley (p.70); Lamb (p.89); Egg (p.92); Bio-yogurt (p.95)

OSTEOPOROSIS

Bone loss occurs as we age, and unless we take the right precautions, we can find ourselves suffering from osteoporosis. A diet rich in calcium is critical for maintaining bone strength throughout life, and vitamin D is also important, as it helps the body to absorb calcium.

Foods to eat:

Cucumber (p.37); Broccoli (p.44); Spinach (p.45); Pumpkin seed (p.67); Flax seed (p.68); Herring (p.86); Haddock (p.87); Oyster (p.88); Milk (p.94); Bio-yogurt (p.95); Parsley (p.99); Ginger (p.100); Cayenne pepper (p.104); Olive oil (p.118)

HEART DISEASE

Along with taking regular cardiovascular exercise, you can go a long way to keeping your heart healthy by avoiding foods containing saturated fats, which raise your cholesterol levels and clog your arteries. Instead, make sure you use healthy monosaturated oils and eat foods containing flavonoids and plenty of fiber.

Foods to eat:

Grape (p.10); Papaya (p.15); Cranberry (p.17); Cantaloupe melon (p.24); Grapefruit (p.27); Pomegranate (p.31); Avocado (p.34); Bell pepper (p.39); Onion (p.41); Broccoli (p.44); Cabbage (p.46); Mushroom (p.52); Asparagus (p.53); Swiss chard (p.55); Almond (p.60); Cashew nut (p.63); Peanut (p.64); Flax seed (p.68); Oats (p.69); Barley (p.70); Soybean (p.78); Sardine (p.82); Oyster (p.88); Green tea (p.96); Garlic (p.98); Fennel (p.102); Coconut oil (p.117)

glossary

Allicin volatile oil found in garlic that may help to suppress tumors

Alpha-hydroxy-acid (AHA) various fruit acids that are capable of trapping moisture in the skin and initiating the formation of collagen, thus helping to prevent the appearance of wrinkles

Anthocyanins dark purple-colored pigments that are antioxidant and aid blood flow

Antioxidant compound that inhibits the effects of harmful free radicals

Arginine organic compound found in animal proteins and peanuts

Astringent acts to draw together, constrict, and bind and is found in skin preparations

Betacyanin crimson pigment found in beet

Bifida bacteria beneficial bacteria that inhabit the intestinal tract and help to fight off infection

Caffeic acid organic acid found in fruits and vegetables

Capsaicin plant chemical found in chilis

Collagen protein central to the maintenance of healthy skin and connective tissue

Conjugated linoleic acid (CLA) naturally occurring fatty acid

Curcumin a potent anti-inflammatory pigment found in turmeric

Cynarin detoxifying, liver-supporting substance

Dimethylaminoethanol (DMAE) chemical compound related to choline, a precursor to the neurotransmitter acetylcholine, and found naturally in fish

Docosahexaenoic acid (DHA) omega-3 fatty acid found in fish oil

Ellagic acid anti-carcinogenic substance found in berries

Ferulic acid antioxidant that protects cells from harmful ultraviolet rays

Flavonoid umbrella term for anti-inflammatory bio-active compounds

Free radicals molecules that damage the body's tissues, produced as a by-product of metabolism or environmental factors

Gamma-linolenic acid (GLA) fatty acid needed for healthy hormone balance, to help lower inflammation and to reduce blood clotting

Glutathione peroxidase enzyme in the body that is a powerful scavenger of free radicals

Hesperidin white or colorless crystalline compound found in citrus fruits

Homocysteine amino acid used normally by the body in cellular metabolism and the manufacture of proteins, but considered a risk factor for several diseases if levels are elevated in the blood

Lactobacillus bacteria, named as such because most of its members convert lactose and other simple sugars to lactic acid

Limonene anti-carcinogenic chemical found in lemons and oranges

Linoleic acid unsaturated fatty acid considered essential to the human diet

Lipoic acid organic acid produced by cells of certain micro-organisms, and essential to processes during metabolism

Lutein antioxidant carotenoid important for eye health

Lycopene antioxidant carotenoid found in red foods

Malic acid tart-tasting organic acid found in apples

Myricetin antioxidant with anti-inflammatory action

Oleic acid oily liquid, and building block for omega-9 fatty acids

Omega-3 and -6 fatty acids polyunsaturated fats found in oily fish, nuts, and seeds

Papain enzyme found in papaya that aids protein digestion

Phenethyl isothiocyanate compound found in vegetables that may be anti-carcinogenic

Phytic acid principal storage form of phosphorus in many plant tissues, especially seeds

Phytochemical plant compound with health-giving properties

Phytoestrogen plant compounds with effects similar to but weaker than those of estrogen

Polyphenol compounds used for chemical synthesis

Quercetin flavonoid with antioxidant properties

Rutin flavonoid for toning and healing peripheral blood vessels

Salicylate salt or ester of salicylic acid; the active substance found in aspirin, and used to treat skin conditions

S-allylcysteine compound found in garlic, said to be anti-carcinogenic

Saponins detoxifying, anti-inflammatory compounds found in herbs, pulses, and vegetables in the plant's outer layer where they form a protective coating

Sulforaphane anti-carcinogenic compound

Terpenes help to produce enzymes that deactivate carcinogens

Tocotrienol antioxidant that comprises vitamin E

Zeaxanthin antioxidant carotenoid important for maintaining eye health

index